SOCIAL SECURITY AND NATIONAL POLICY

Social Security and National Policy

SWEDEN

YUGOSLAVIA

JAPAN

David E. Woodsworth

McGill–Queen's University Press
MONTREAL AND LONDON 1977

© McGill–Queen's University Press 1977
ISBN 0 7735 0282 3 (cloth)
      0 7735 0283 1 (paper)
Legal deposit second quarter 1977
Bibliothèque Nationale du Québec

Printed in Canada by
Imprimerie Gagné Ltée

CONTENTS

Part V Conclusion

TABLES

JAPAN

CHARTS

Part 1

Introduction

CHAPTER ONE

Alternative Approaches to Social Benefits

The Justification of Social Welfare Benefits

The phrase "quiet revolution" is most often used in Canada to refer to Quebec's emergence as a self-conscious political, economic, and cultural unit: one among Canada's provinces, but "pas comme les autres." A similar quiet revolution has occurred throughout the world, especially in the decades since the second World War, in the establishment of social security as a political and economic fact. The farsighted assessment, predictions, and recommendations on social security in Canada made by Leonard Marsh in 1943 have been sustained and carried forward.[1] Step by step, Canada has moved to put in place a series of provisions for protection to many groups in the population against a whole range of contingencies, and to elaborate, strengthen, or modify the provisions as needs change. Like most modern nations, Canada has developed programs to aid special categories of people who are unemployable or unemployed, or general categories of people such as old persons or children, or the total population, as in the case of health care. The Marsh report has provided a kind of master list, with the rationale for adoption of many of these programs over thirty years.

As recognized by Marsh, the relationship of employment to social benefits has always been significant, and it continues to be a key element in most social benefit programs. It is expressed most recently even in the proposals for a form of "guaranteed income" accepted by Canadian federal and provincial welfare ministers in 1976. That proposal, borrowed from the "Castonguay Commission" report is based on a two-step plan distinguishing between the needs of employable or employed workers on low income, and those of unemployable people.[2] This program, like most, is designed in the light of its effect on, or as an outcome of, the individual's behaviour in the labour market, or on the state of the labour market itself, and so is not a "guarantee" at all—or no more so than centuries-old public welfare.

The influence of the labour market on social security is expressed in many ways. Benefits are often dependent on contributions, or on the individual's earnings, or on his work history; or they may be related to minimum wage levels, or to income taxes that are related to earnings, and so on. Programs have also sometimes been used as economic instruments. They may have been intended (as in the case of family allowances) as a hedge against economic recession by the distribution of spending power. In general, a guiding principle has been that these programs should stimulate or help to regulate the economy but should not interfere with the operation of the labour market. In addition to their economic uses, they have political values. At election time there is recurrent reference, depending on the state of the economy, to increasing the benefits of deserving old people, or, alternatively, to getting rid of "welfare bums." An increase in old age pensions is a familiar promise made by contenders for power. Social security programs thus reflect political and economic objectives as much as they do attitudes about or concern for people in need.

The history of the development of social security in Canada is similar to that of other western industrialized nations. Indeed there are such similarities among nations that the International Labour Organization, through its agency the International Social Security Association, is able to publish comparative reports in which the same terminology and concepts are generally applicable. Borrowing, in fact, may account for a good many of the similarities; the expectations of the ILO itself no doubt account for some of it. Furthermore, as Heclo notes, national bureaucracies share common obligations, roles, and orientations, so that their communication facilitates the borrowing process.[3]

Comparative studies of national social security programs are not infrequent, since nations are always looking for improvement, and these comparisons often examine in general the cost of social security, or of specific programs, as a proportion of Gross National Product.[4] It is possible to argue, as Harold Wilensky has very ably done, that the best indicator of a nation's commitment to social security is the proportion of GNP spent on all social security programs.[5] He recognizes, however, that a significant part of the allocation is determined by costs related to the age of the population and to the age (or maturity) of widely used and expensive programs like old age pensions. He discounts the influence of national political and philosophical traditions in the development of programs, placing emphasis on economic capacity and economic policy as determinants of welfare policy. Granted that the general thrust of social security is the same everywhere, in that the same problems are addressed, the same populations protected, and that expenditures must be related to the nation's capacity to pay for them, there remain critical differences in such areas as coverage, conditions of eligibility, the breadth and diversity of benefits, and the location of responsibility for costs, which must be explained. It is our argument that they can only be explained by national political goals and values. Is it not significant, for example, that the United States still has no universal health care program, long after most other modern but less affluent nations have adopted it?

Wilensky's position suggests that affluence "causes" good social security programs. But that is most evident if good results are measured by expenditure rather than by other factors, such as distribution of income powers. As will be seen, Sweden devotes great attention to searching out and meeting inadequacies in a complex and exhaustive social security system, and is concerned with equalization of benefits, or with "social justice" more than with individual compensation. This passion for social justice may account for affluence, as well as the converse. That is, in fact, an explicit argument used in Yugoslavia to jusitfy policies of self-management of industry.

The similarities and differences among nations may also be examined in relation to the processes of policy-making and administration. Comparisons of social security programs usually focus on the provisions of the programs rather than on their administration, but forms of administration not only influence the provisions, but are a source of satisfaction (or dissatisfaction) in themselves. Satisfaction is measured not only by the results of bureaucratic efficiency, but as the bureaucrats successfully or otherwise interpret the needs and attitudes of the nation. Public attitudes are embedded in the total complex of social institutions, values, and images of the people, and are therefore not easily transplanted to other nations. It is the complexity of the relationship of social security programs to other national institutions that makes it difficult to assume the determining place of economic variables in their development, and that kindles interest in comparison of administration as well as of other components of social security.

In summary, due acknowledgement must be given to the financial limits to a nation's ability to provide social security, and the borrowing of ideas among nations is evident. But not only do the differences remain among nations in the details of programs; national programs become consistent with and reinforce each other in such a way as to reveal distinct national packages that reflect national cultural traditions, politics, and geography at least as much as they do national economics. The preservation and development of work, or employment, remains in all nations a central principle around which both the provisions of social security programs and their administration are organized. This is so not only because of the economic value of work to the nation, but also, apparently, because of its meaning to the worker and to others in society. Given the universal centrality of productive employment, nations nonetheless give it different weight, and these differences are expressed in social security provisions.

The process of standardization of terminology by such bodies as the ILO has made it possible to classify programs according to major components. But such classification may induce unwarranted attributions of shared purposes and philosophy, and a warning must accordingly be given. Programs that bear the same designations and hold the same ostensible purposes are often quite different in origin, operation, and outcomes. Or old programs are given new names. For example, unemployment insurance plays a very much smaller part in Yugoslavia than in Canada, though the unemployment rates are about the same. This suggests political rather than economic factors.

The Comparison of Programs

In order to get behind the surface resemblances of national programs, it seems desirable to look more closely at the relationships of social security programs to each other and their relationship to the political and cultural traditions of the nation. To this end, three countries were selected for study: Sweden, Yugoslavia, and Japan; Sweden because of its socialist politics, capitalist economy, and industrial success; Yugoslavia because of its decentralized communist politics and style of industrial self-management; Japan because of the paternalistic, technologically efficient and integrated management of both government and industry. Despite these major differences, it will be seen that all tend to look for collective solutions to social needs. Two main areas of focal interest emerge: first to see how social programs relate to the countries' ways of organizing work, and second, to examine the management of the social benefit programs, and especially the relationship of the bureaucracy to political authorities and to consumers, for management forms directly reflect political and economic attitudes in the country.

In addition to questions of management, we have noted four main substantive areas that engage the attention of students of social security. These are coverage, the terms of eligibility, contributions, and benefits.[6] These all reflect assumptions and intentions about the relation of the individual to society. The absolute level of benefits as such is not as indicative as are the kind of benefits or the level of benefits relative to average incomes, for the actual amounts of course vary with the country's affluence more than with the attitudes about work.[7] The relative levels of benefit do, however, reveal the society's valuation of the status of the recipient, as do the manner of financing, and rules on the limits of eligibility and on the intended groups to be served. We shall be more concerned here with relative than with absolute distributions. These four areas become the "nuts and bolts" of comparison.

In what terms are programs to be compared or evaluated? Surely not, in the long run, by measures of efficiency, or statistics on the proportion of GNP devoted to social programs, but by the extent to which they satisfy the expectations of the people in a society. Those expectations are expressions of wants, and perhaps basically of needs, especially in respect to material needs, safety or security, and the sense of self-fulfilment. These three kinds of needs are met through two kinds of mechanisms in every society: mechanisms for the distribution of goods, and for the distribution of roles and statuses (or social rights). In terms of social programs, they refer to the distribution of costs and benefits, and to the distribution and interrelation of roles of contributors, beneficiaries, and policy-makers. The main questions to be asked are: "How equally are goods and powers distributed? What is the relationship of the distribution to work experience? How widely in the population are benefits distributed? Does the acquisition of some benefits and powers give an advantage for the acquisition of more?" These are questions of fact. Whether these distributions *should* be as they are are questions of value and will vary with the countries concerned.

Given the need to measure all three, satisfaction of material needs, security, and fulfilment, on what dimensions should they be measured? If "equality" is taken as a test of value, programs can be measured first by the breadth of distribution of resources and powers among the population (measures of coverage, in social security terms); second, by the degree of equality or inequality among participants in the amounts of benefits or in the access to decision-making power; and third, by the degree to which resources and roles are dispersed among persons or concentrated in certain individuals. There is no necessary "right" way to satisfy people in diverse cultures; equality or participation are not necessarily expected in all societies. However, the satisfaction of common perceptions of "appropriate" distribution is taken as essential in all cultures. The question that emerges is, how do different societies satisfy expectations regarding what people see as the proper distribution of resources and power? The answer must lie in the relationships between economic and political systems, and the roles assigned to the worker or the nonworker in these two systems.

Daniel Bell says, "In western political systems the axial problem is the relation between the desire for popular participation and bureaucracy."[8] This is proposed in the context of his observation that the problems of postindustrial society are those of services, of interpersonal management, rather than the management of industrial production. The question of the organization or management of social security, the allocation of roles in the social security system, and in particular the strain between popular participation and bureaucracy in the development and management of services is thus of central concern. If the role of bureaucracy is as strong as Heclo suggests, it becomes very important to clarify the authority to which the bureaucracy is accountable. The question is not limited to western societies in a geographic sense, but should be applied to all societies with advanced technologies, including Japan. There is no reason, furthermore, to limit the question to countries with advanced technologies. Yugoslavia is not relatively advanced in industrial technology, but is concerned perhaps more than any other nation with the strain between participation and bureaucracy. It seems then that popular participation may not be a matter of focal interest even in an advanced society, but may be so in one that is less advanced. The explanation of these exceptions to Bell's general proposition seems to be that important as are technological and economic factors in shaping political forms, both are located in the larger realities of history, culture, and geography, and reflect them.

It seems useful, in summary, to ask how satisfying to the people concerned are the ways material resources and decision-making powers are in fact distributed. How do political and economic powers relate to each other in these decisions? What are the channels by which workers or nonworkers have access to decisions on the amounts and processes of allocation of resources, and what are the benefits resulting? What follows, then, is a description of the administration and provisions of social security and other social programs in three countries, focusing on the patterns each has adopted towards satisfaction of needs of income, security, and self-realization through the distribution of incomes and of the costs, benefits, and powers of control of social programs.

Income and its Measurement

Income is usually thought of as money received from any source, for any reason. But especially when discussing social benefits, it is necessary to recognize that income means more than money. Increasingly, social benefits are received in the form of goods and services. Sometimes these goods cannot, in their nature, be bought by individuals, or at least are bought at great inconvenience. Examples are police, postal, and fire services, sewage and water, public thoroughfares, and, notwithstanding some advocates of private services, education and preventive health. Other services have more recently come into the public sphere, notably health care and housing.

Income, or wealth, has always tended to be cumulative. "To him who hath shall be given." For a variety of reasons, no country has equalized incomes or benefits, beyond setting rather wide-ranging minimum and maximum limits. In calculating social benefits in their major programs, most countries have used a percentage of income or of average wages, and the disparities of earned incomes are thus perpetuated in disparities of benefits. One alternative route has been the flat-rate benefit that characterized the Beveridge plan in Great Britain and various programs in other countries (like family allowances and old age security in Canada). This has not been successful because the flat rate has always been kept at a low level both for reasons of cost and (as for Beveridge) so as not to interfere with work motivation. Therefore many countries adopt a composite system combining flat-rate and work-related benefits.

Services, like incomes, have been cumulative as opportunities for their use increase with income and related social status. However, one of the reasons for the introduction of social benefits and especially benefits in kind is to assure basic standards, and possibly to moderate the effect of cumulative differences.

At least two difficulties arise in estimating equalization trends, or in comparing the programs of different countries. One is that in programs offering benefits or services in kind (such as health care and housing) it is hard to estimate the qualitative differences, or to reduce them to quantitative terms. It is hard to say without detailed study, whether rich people get better medical care than poor people in a health insurance program.

Another difficulty is that while a number of factors affect income distribution, different countries put different emphasis, for purposes of policy-making, on these factors. Experts have often recognized the difficulty of making intercountry comparisons because of this; data are not comparable, because they have been prepared for a variety of purposes. The income variables tabulated in the general statistics available from Yugoslavia, Sweden, and Japan differ in significant ways. Yugoslavia reports income by industry, level of skill of the worker, and family size. Sweden reports by type of industry, age, and marital status. Japan puts emphasis on the type of industry and size of firm. All countries recognize the difference between male and female workers, but there are revealing differences between Sweden and Japan.

It is well known that both education and sex are closely related to type of job and income level. Age is usually of less importance, and family size and marital status are usually not regarded. Many questions of policy can be raised around whether these factors should affect income, but cannot be answered by reference to statistics. The best than can be done as a beginning is to report on the basis of the information presented by each country and the priorities that are evidenced.

Social Benefits

The term "social benefits" has been used almost interchangeably here with "social programs," mainly to avoid use of the term "social security." The reason is that the latter term is used by authorities in the field to define a limited and specific group of programs that include and even hinge upon the principle of insurance, or user contributions. This is the limited meaning applied by the International Social Security Association. Most of the programs discussed here come within that limitation, but some do not. The reason was suggested above: that such benefits are increasingly moving into services that may not conveniently (or justly) be charged to the user. The insurance principle is only one possible way of meeting individual or collective needs, and for some needs it is not even appropriate. The term social security is therefore not broad enough to cover all of the programs that make up national packages of income support or other benefits.

Some of the underlying issues in the choice of programs have already been touched on. Detailed discussion of principles is found in many other places,[9] and attention may be drawn only to the main issues that have engaged social policy-makers in debate over many decades, and that are indicated in the discussion to follow, on each country.

Coverage. Should programs be selective or categorical (usually relative to employability), or should they be universal? That is, should they apply to certain predefined categories of people on the basis of their capacities and needs (such as the disabled and the blind), or should they apply to everyone in a major group regardless of need, such as all children up to age 16, or all adults over 65? If they are to be selective, who should be excluded, and on what grounds? There are both economic and moral arguments in favour of selectivity. But if these are conceded in the face of need (as is done now very generally) the main argument in favour of selectivity is that resources are applied efficiently to a target, helping those in need without incurring large costs. Against this is the moral and psychological problem of stigmatizing the recipient by requiring proof of incapacity (or failure). Universality avoids stigma but involves paying benefits to those who do not need it. It is argued that taxation of incomes can recover the cost of payments to the rich; but there are advantages for the rich in most tax systems that may still leave the balance of benefit with them.

Other kinds of program selectivity arise from differences in the kind of industry, or the level of wages, or the age or sex of the worker. For example, some programs exclude certain kinds of workers. In most countries, these are seasonal or casual workers, or those in agriculture, forestry, or fishing, whose employment may be erratic and whose contributions therefore are difficult to estimate and collect. In short, strict application of the insurance principle excludes many of those who may need it most. This may apply to unemployment insurance, pensions, or sick benefit.

Similarly, workers who have less than a certain minimum income may be "exempted": that is, excluded, because of their inability to make contributions. Another kind of exclusion may be based on the ownership of the enterprise. This may be at the same time related to the size of enterprise or kind of work. In Yugoslavia, for example, farmers in cooperatives may be covered for health and pension insurance, but not individual farmers. It might be argued that selective exclusion can work to the benefit of a needy group of people by concentrating resources to their service, but matters do not work that way. Stigma attaches in all societies to the nonworker, and social benefits are never much above the level that can be earned by work. Universal programs, on the other hand, must satisfy both workers and nonworkers, and people at every income level. This does not necessarily mean equalization, but at least attention can be given to comparison of benefits received by different groups in the population, so that the issues of equality can be examined, as they tend not to be in selective programs.

Eligibility. "Coverage" by a program does not mean that a person is eligible to benefits. Very often there are minimum and maximum boundaries. The limits may refer to allowable income or assets. That is, eligibility may be conditional on the applicant's income, or means, or assets, or simply on estimated needs relative to means. Or eligibility may depend on the individual having contributed a minimum amount of money over a minimum amount of time, or in a certain sequence. Or it may depend (as in the case of disability) on a certain degree of physical or mental disability. Or it may depend on age, or upon a degree of family relationship or consanguinity. It may depend upon the political or legal jurisdiction in which one lives, or upon citizenship, or upon the time one has resided in a jurisdiction. In northern Europe, a major problem in social policy has been the coverage and eligibility for social benefits of so-called guest workers from other countries (such as Yugoslavia).

All of these limitations or boundaries to eligibility may be used to restrict or expand use, thus regulating costs and differentials of income or other benefits.

Contributions. The issue of contributions, and in particular the relation of contributions to benefits, is of course at the heart of insurance. The ideal of insurance is that the contributor pays an insurer at a sufficient rate that the insurer can afford to repay the contributor if the event at risk occurs. There are many difficulties in achieving the ideal in social insurance. One factor is that some of the "risks" are not risks but certainties (such as old age and death) or are so common that the cost of insuring would be equal to the cost of the event. Another is that those most in need of help are those least able to pay for it. Thus the unemployed man may be ineligible for unemployment insurance because he did not work long enough to establish his credit.

There is a tendency for social insurance to move away from dependence on individual contributions, to the assignment to employers or governments of increasing proportions of the cost, and away from the establishment of large reserve funds to acceptance of pay-as-you-go taxation. This trend is encouraged by recognition (as noted earlier) that unemployment and loss of income are at least as much collective as individual problems.

The central issues around contributions have to do with the proportions to be paid by workers as insured individuals, by employers, and by the state. Usually the amounts are fixed as a percentage of the individual's wage, or of the company payroll, up to a maximum that presumably represents the upper limit of an "average" wage. The state then makes up a fixed proportion, or the balance needed.

The contributions are in effect a form of tax, and the question is how much of that tax should be borne by the person at risk, or by the economic organizations from which the society's wealth derives in any case, or whether the risk should be spread among all economic sources through overt taxation.

A related question is whether contributions should be at a fixed rate for all, or should vary according to use, or "experience," or according to capacity to pay. This question relates in turn to the source of contributions. If individual users were to pay according to their use, those with most trouble would pay most. On the other hand, variable charges have been made again at employers in some countries (including Japan), in unemployment insurance, on the basis of their turnover rates. Where employment or unemployment is at the employer's decision, such a policy may be useful. In general, however, experience-rated charges contradict the principle of sharing risks, especially where those risks are not at the control of the contributor.

A more difficult question is whether contribution rates should vary with personal income level, at least where contributions are based on individual incomes. A percentage of individual income is common as a basis for calculating contributors, and up to a point this means a modified progressive tax rate. But the rate almost never increases with income, beyond a maximum level to which the tax applies, so that higher income levels remain untaxed. In this sense a fixed-rate tax is regressive. Yet this is the general pattern. The issue does not arise where contributions are paid by employers as a percentage of total payroll. Different countries give different answers to these questions according to their view of the degree to which societal relations are contractual or systemic, of the part played by individual motivations and accepted concepts of fairness, and of the relationships of employers and the State.

Social Benefits.   The questions to be asked about benefits have to do with relative quantities and quality. How much benefit can be received in relation to contributions? Should benefits relate to the individual's wage, or to an average wage for some special work group, or to an average for all workers? Should all receive a flat rate of benefits? The answers to such questions indicate the stand a country takes on the principle of equalization. If equalization is not a goal, there need be no concern about differences in contribution rates, or relating benefits directly to widely varying individual contributions. On the other hand, a flat benefit is not the answer, as was discovered in Britain by those who revised the Beveridge plan. Flat benefits are usually set at too low a rate to avoid serious material and psychological disadvantages for the recipients. Rather, certain groups most in need may require un-equally high benefits to help them get out of habitual difficulties. Benefits related to individual wages do not satisfy this need for special aid; therefore programs that aspire to equalization need to relate bene-fits to the average for all workers or at least to large groups of workers, even though the latter choice leaves room for large disparities.

Whether or not equalization is the goal, the question, in all cases, is what proportion of the average wage, whichever average is used, should be met? The answer seems to depend on the view that is taken, first of the purpose of the program, and second of the effect of bene-fits on the recipients' motivation or self-perception. The purpose may be counter to equalization, that is, to maintain the recipient at a mini-mal or subsistence level, on the indifferent principles either that he will be moved to take action for self-help, or that he is already so use-less that further aid would not result in change. This is often the apparent philosophy of noncontributory programs and of many old age and survivors' pensions. Or the purpose may be to equalize: to keep the recipient close to (or raise him to) the average level of living (and self-respect) of his community, in the expectation that he will be moved to keep up those levels of living and respect if possible, or that if he cannot do so, he should not be punished for an involuntary failure. Unemployment, disability, and sickness insurances often fit this category. Or, finally, the purpose of the program may be elitist: to provide benefit at a level even higher than the average, on the ground that special rehabilitation is needed to recreate the recipient's productivity, or that the individual's past or potential social contri-bution is so great that it deserves extraordinary investment by society. The last category is well represented by programs for civil servants and academics. (One wonders why assumptions about human moti-vation change at this level.) In most countries, programs are rather consistent in purpose and effect, perhaps combining the first and last perspectives, which are both counter-equalization. In Canada, we do in fact use both of the other two principles.

Management. The main issues around management of social benefit programs have to do with (1) the extent to which programs are pre-scribed by governments and administered by them; (2) whether ad-ministered by governments or other authorities, the extent to which administrative decisions are centralized, or are dispersed among smaller authorities; and (3) the mechanisms for representation of user interests in either centralized or decentralized authorities.

These questions have to do with how far policy-making roles co-incide with the roles of contributor and user. Governments may simply pass enabling legislation, assigning broad responsibility for both policy-making and administration to other bodies, or they may prescribe procedures in detailed regulations and then either carry out administration through their own ministries and civil service or assign implementation of details to administrative agencies with narrowly limited authority. Depending on the country, government policy may be initiated by parliament or a cabinet, or it may be initiated at local levels of interest groups or users and be passed to legislatures for approval. There is, in short, a wide range of possibilities for the creation and application of policy, from highly centralized political authority and large bureaucracy, to widely decentralized political action and local administrative autonomy. The mechanisms for either pattern are varied. There is no right or wrong way, but some come closer than others to equalization of powers through dispersal of roles.

The Choice of Countries

The three countries chosen for examination are very different on many counts, though all have strongly collectivistic goals and structures. In population, Japan has about 108 million people, Yugoslavia about 21 million and Sweden about 8 million. Japan and Sweden are racially and culturally homogeneous, politically centralist with one senior government, and are among the most disciplined and successful industrial states in the world. They are, however, very different in their approach to the distribution of incomes and roles. Japan appears to assume and accept marked differences and to develop policy around them, while Sweden explicitly seeks consistently to reduce them. Yugoslavia is composed of six autonomous republics, representing several distinct ethnic and linguistic groups with divergent traditions. It is in the process of change from an agricultural to an industrial nation, with marked differences among regions in that process. Differences are recognized, but treated as contrary to the nation's organizing principle of local autonomy and participation. All three countries are earnestly seeking means for the achievement of national goals that are consonant with their own characters, all are trying to express these means in terms of the rights and duties of individuals, and more specifically in terms of incomes and social benefits, and of the individual's part in work and politics.

Given the differences in political and cultural characteristics, the social security programs of the three countries are remarkably similar and comparable in expressed purpose and structure. All have health care, cash sickness benefits, pensions for retirement, disability, and survivors, unemployment insurance, workmen's accident and illness compensation, children's allowances, work-training programs, housing allowances, and general social assistance. Yet in all of these programs there are differences in coverage, eligibility, contributions, and benefits, and in the structures for management. The goals and distributive outcomes are different. The differences in management, or control of social benefits are not necessarily reflected in the level of benefits as such, or even in coverage or terms of eligibility, which vary with the state of development of each program and generally of the nation. Managerial principles are more likely to be revealed in contributions formulae or financing arrangements, and, above all, merit examination in themselves as indicative of attitudes about the relation of the worker to both economic and political systems.

Yugoslavia's management and financing of social resources of all kinds is closely interwoven with management of economic and political affairs, requiring the participation of large numbers of people. Bureaucracies tend to be local, therefore small, and accountable to local political forces. Contributions to social security are in principle scarcely distinguishable from resources allocated on the one hand to economic objectives or on the other to other social programs, such as education. In most capitalist countries there are sharp distinctions between programs that are seen as serving common goals, such as education, which are collectively financed and governed by public authority, and those that are seen as primarily serving the individual, such as contributory social security programs. Political and administrative processes vary accordingly. Individual contributions in western systems are often compulsorily deducted at source and deposited in a central fund with no decision required of the "contributor," yet are regarded as personal investments leading to certain entitlements. In Yugoslavia, deductions are made even further back, being collected as a percentage of the total payroll without reference to individual salaries, and so are embedded in the national product. Individual entitlement is guaranteed by collective decision and by law, not by personal investment. Management of social funds, including the setting of contributions and benefits, becomes the business of local collective organizations of contributors and users. The goal of policy is to effect both wide dispersion and correlation of roles, to involve as many people as possible in the related activities of contribution, use, and management of benefits. In this sense, Yuogoslavia, though torn by uncertainty about political and economic means and by internal rifts, represents a systemic approach to social policy.

In Sweden, management is largely centralized, with collective responsibility assigned to state-approved boards. The exception is unemployment insurance, which is managed by unions or other employee associations. Policy is determined jointly by central representatives of organized labour, organized employers, and government. Power is not dispersed to many persons, but is shared among power blocks that represent many persons. Contributions to programs reflect this balance, or mixture of capitalism and socialism. Workers do not contribute to pensions directly, but do contribute directly to health insurance and unemployment insurance. Employers do not contribute directly to unemployment insurance, but do contribute to health insurance and pensions. Employers in addition make substantial contributions to supplementary insurance programs and other fringe benefits, through consultation and negotiation with unions. A major effort is made to reduce disparities in benefits, by extending eligibility not only among workers, but now also to nonworkers. While maintaining a strong basis of individual contributions, Sweden seems to have set herself to extend security to the entire population, working or not, on the principle that a healthy nation cannot afford inequality of treatment among its people. In this sense, Sweden too takes a systemic rather than contractual approach to social policy.

Japan, most closely of the three countries considered here, approximates the Canadian, or more exactly the United States position. Superficially the system is individualistic in concept. More fundamentally, government is seen to exercise control in detail, and responsibility in detail, through employers. Contributions are shared in all major insurance programs, by employers, employees, and the state. Individual noncontributors are assured only minimal residual benefits by the state. Benefit levels vary widely, based on contributions. The management of programs does not call for the participation of users, being carried either by the central government or by employers' associations. Employers also unilaterally offer many substantial fringe benefits, without worker paritcipation. Economic policy and even social policy responds primarily to the views of employers, especially large employers, but is moderated by the technocratic power of central government bureaucracy. This does not mean that social security is denied to Japanese workers. On the contrary, most workers are assured of basic material security in the job as well as in times of need. But there are noteworthy differences in outcomes of benefits, and a well-defined hierarchy of roles within a rigid structure of authority.

Japan exhibits both contractual and systemic characteristics. Highly competitive within the country as in its relations with other countries, politically centralized, and accepting of a sharply vertical social and economic structure, it nonetheless shares deeply felt goals and values of collective unity and purpose. While the collective goals of Sweden and Yugoslavia are to equalize, those of Japan retain inequality.

These then are the themes that have guided this enquiry. No claim is made to have provided here quantitative proofs of the distribution or equalization of benefits, or of correlations in the allocation of benefits or powers. Such studies are being done by experts in each country as part of national policy-making. It is hoped only that the descriptions that follow will give some indication of the trends in each country and some suggestions of useful policy for others.

Part 2

Sweden

CHAPTER TWO

Sweden: The People, The State

Some nations project more clearly than others images of themselves in the minds of other people, because of their achievements in certain fields or because of their racial and cultural distinctiveness. Sweden is one of these. These self-images are expressed in political and economic choices, and in Sweden, social security policies are prominent among the choices. Sweden is almost the prototype of the welfare state. Without attempting an explanation and at the risk of repeating a stereotype, it is useful to sketch the outlines of the Swedish image and some of the major decision-making structures.

THE PEOPLE

The Swedes are self-consciously hard-working, purposeful, practical, efficient. They value integrity, personal responsibility, social commitment, equality, and justice. They value logic, order, and intellectual achievement. Sometimes the relentless pursuit of these virtues creates a sense of oppression and revulsion even among the Swedes, who may long to experience, at least sometimes, the sense of irresponsibility, or to let emotions take priority over intellect. Lutheranism is the state religion. With typical consistency, churches are supported by taxes, and are kept in excellent condition, in contrast with the desperate state of many churches in other lands. But they are empty.

Truth is sought through rational self-discipline on a national scale. Critics of the welfare state may take pleasure in quoting suicide rates or sexual behaviour in Sweden, but such factors reflect not so much a removal of challenge as the inescapability of an existential, personal responsibility.

Racially, Sweden is remarkably homogeneous, with a population of only just over eight million. There have been many "guest workers" (including large numbers of Yugoslavs). About 5 percent of residents are foreign citizens, but like other northern European countries, Sweden does not encourage permanent immigrants. By comparison, Canada's relatively open door (or at least swinging door) policy is thought by some Swedes to be fatal to the creation of a sound and stable social policy. Knowing its own people, Sweden can create long-term policies, based on predictable values and political behaviour.

As a result, Sweden is remarkably stable politically. For over forty years it had a Social Democratic government strongly favourable to organized labour and committed to social equality and social welfare. Though Sweden has several political parties, national policies have become so fully expressed in political and administrative structures and processes that it would be almost unthinkable that any government would wish to or be able to make substantial changes in direction.

It is important to note, too, that Sweden is a unitary state, with considerable centralization of responsibility and power. There is no dispute over jurisdiction, as there is in Canada between federal and provincial governments. This does not mean that Sweden is undemocratic. It has other means of distributing both political and administrative powers, that may convey more real participation than does Canada's reliance on representative government at three levels.

THE STRUCTURES AND PROCESSES OF GOVERNMENT

Political Parties

There are five major parties in Sweden: Conservative, Liberal, Center, Social Democratic Labour and Left/Communist. Parliament is elected by proportional representation. That is, each party is represented according to its proportion of the popular vote, thus ensuring a political voice to a variety of points of view. In the British system, where the life of government depends on majority vote in the House, and therefore on strict party discipline, this system could lead to political instability. While the responsibility for government in Sweden is also assigned to the party with the greatest representation, the loss of a vote in the House does not spell the fall of government. Cabinet solidarity is not essential to the survival of government, and individual cabinet members may be censured or dismissed. There is more room for and need for coalitions and public discussion.

Sweden has used its political powers and the known values of its people to create a consistent, disciplined state whose first concern is the welfare of its people. Economic and human resources are employed to that end. New experiments in the democratization of industry are being actively pursued, making use of the aspirations and motivations of the workers within the context of collective or social goals. Democracy in the work place is extending from decisions about working conditions and benefits to decisions about the organization of production. The same values and goals are found, then, in work, in politics, and in personal or community life.

In Sweden, there has in fact been great political stability, possibly because the government is not directly responsible for administration. Further, stability is due in considerable part to the fact that both labour and management are disciplined, with a balance of power and agreement on common aims of productivity that override and control excess on either side.

Public Accountability

Two or three other political processes seem significant to the success of Swedish policies. One is the "remiss" process, whereby wide use is made of consultation of opposition parties, administrative organs, and organizations of the public. Royal commissions are common, and proposals are presented for public discussion before being put into legislaiton. The use of legislative committees as vehicles for public discussion is gradually growing in Canada, but the Swedish practice goes even further by actively soliciting opinions of concerned bodies. This principle of consultation is observed down through local government and in the operation of nongovernment organizations.

A second and related process is the rule of publicity, whereby all documents directed to or coming from government or public agencies are open for inspection (with safeguards for limited areas like national defence). The press appears to take its role very seriously, watching for, analysing, and publishing information. This practice is in marked contrast and opposition to most bureaucratic procedures. In Canada it is often impossible for ciitzens to have access to the mountains of "confidential" government documents concerning policies in process of formation.

On the same principle is the well-known institution of ombudsman and various appeal provisions that give the citizen defence or recourse against bad treatment by official bodies or individuals. And yet another is the personal responsibility of public officials for their acts, so that from a minister of the crown down to a local clerk, they may be called to account for any injury done to a person who might expect their help or service. Punishment may range from criticism or reprimand to loss of job, fine, or imprisonment. At the same time, public servants are assured of tenure unless found guilty of an offence, and are not subject to changes of government or political direction.

The success of all these institutionalized practices depends of course on their acceptance by most Swedish citizens. In operation they emphasize the individual values of equality of treatment and mutual responsibility. However, they are not the same thing as grass-roots control or worker management, nor do they depend on the energy or concern of individuals alone. Fair play is assured within formalized structures, where worker representation is matched by law with employer representation. Indeed, success seems to depend on maintaining a balance of political and economic power between labour and management, which has developed over several decades, and which is embedded in public aministration as well as in industry. It is by such institutions that the distribution of power is assured over time.

Administrative Democracy

Economically, Sweden remains a capitalist country. But democracy at work becomes increasingly inseparable from political democracy, both because of the generalization and habitual use of democratic principles, and because the distinction between work-related benefits and the benefits available to all citizens become less and less significant politically. Industry is increasingly seen as a social resource, as the source of benefits for the whole nation. It is not surprising that a major public issue is not so much whether the management of industry should be transferred from private to public hands, but the relative contribution that can be made to the use of these social resources by private owners and organized labour.

The lines of decision regarding industrial democracy are already forecast by well-established patterns of public administration. Unity of policy is assured in Sweden by centralization of political and administrative power, but that power is distributed in three ways: first, by the separation of political authority and administrative responsibility; second, by formal representation of major power blocs, especially employers and unions, in administrative bodies; and, third, by the delegation of administrative responsibility to representative regional bodies.

In both the British and American systems of government, major public programs are administered by bureaucracies headed by politicians and their appointees, who are accountable to the cabinet and/or the chief executive. A great deal of debate occurs over the accuracy of the descriptions of politicians as exclusive policy-makers and bureaucrats as efficient but anonymous servants. Political futures depend upon the politician's ability to justify his administration, and therefore upon his control of his bureaucrats.

In Sweden, as in several other North European countries, while legislation and policy are indeed the business of politicians, administration of most major programs is delegated to boards. The managers of boards are appointed by government, but the boards themselves represent major economic and social interests. Needless to say, the boards contribute to the formation of policy, not just to its interpretation. The separation of political and administrative power, so significant in the modern Swedish program of redistribution, was achieved as long ago as the Constitution of 1720, and is deeply embedded in Swedish political thought.[1] Such boards include those for education, social welfare, health and pension insurance, housing, and the labour market. One of the most active and influential is the Labour Market Board. It deserves some elaboration because of the relationship of employment to social benefits.

The National Labour Market Board

The National Labour Market Board carries responsibility for planning and operation of the nation's manpower programs, including job creation, employment, training, mobility, and supervision of unemployment insurance, combining most of the functions of Canada's Departments of Labour and Manpower. The National Board consists of a director general, his deputy, and eleven members who are appointed by the government, upon the recommendation of the Swedish Employers' Confederation (for 3), the Confederation of Swedish Trade Unions (3), the Central Organization of Salaried Employees (2), the Swedish Confederation of Professional Associations (1), female labour (1), and agriculture (1).

The work of the board at the local level is carried out by 24 "county" labour boards. These are not a direct part of county government, but local agents of the National Board chaired by the county governors. At this county level, too, the boards consist of representatives of employers and trade unions in proportions similar to those at the national level. There are also district employment offices working under the county boards, with special committees and frequent contacts among unions, employment offices, and employers about the employment of special groups. The boards are not accountable to the labour minister or cabinet, except in a general sense within the terms of their empowering legislation.

The staffing of the boards is important. Many of the staff are themselves union members, who have gone through a period of training for the job. Their identification is usually with the applicant for work or training, who is seen as the client, rather than with the employer, or with the government. They are workers first, bureaucrats second.

Unemployment insurance is supervised by the National Labour Market Board, but is operated by unions: a situation that Canadian ministers may envy, given the political explosiveness of unemployment insurance. The unions have been pressed to turn over administration to the board, but resist this move on the ground that their control keeps them directly informed of the state of the labour market and of the efficiency of the board. They do work closely with the county boards, since the claimant must register for employment with the boards. The union may refuse to grant insurance if they are not satisfied about the claim. It is not necessary to be a union member to belong to the unemployment insurance association, but the great majority of industrial workers are unionized. The unemployment insurance program is in effect operated by the users, and their strength relative to the Labour Market Board ensures good treatment in the administration of the board's widespread programs.

The assurance of job security is increasingly demanded in modern nations, undergirding social security. This principle was reasserted in the European ILO Conference of 1974, stressing job protection.[2] In Sweden, one of several major recent advances in job security was an "Act Concerning Employment Security," that came into force 1 July 1974. The worker's right to a job is specified, and the employer's right to fire is sharply limited. There must be "cause" for firing, and if there is a dispute on this point, the union may negotiate. During this time, the worker remains on full pay. However, discharges may occur because of production cutbacks and in this case the order of firing is based on seniority and age. New policy has also been set in such areas as occupational safety, and insistence on work opportunities for handicapped people. The government subsidizes firms to make this possible. The place of union shop stewards responsible for safety is clarified and counted as legitimate activity on company time. Union representatives are assured seats on boards of directors hiring over 100 workers.[3] In all these ways, and more, the workplace is "democratized," and the influence of this process extends into national and local politics and into the administration of public programs including social security.

The National Social Insurance Board and Services

Boards have different composition according to their functions. The National Social Insurance Board has considerable central authority for standard setting, operation of pensions at the national level including establishing the contribution rates for social insurance. However, local administration of pensions, health insurance, industrial injuries, and supplementary pensions is carried out by twenty-seven autonomous local funds or associations at the level of the county. Local social insurance boards are representative; one member is appointed by the central government, one by the national board, one by the county administration, and four by the county council or town councils. There is, in addition, the National Insurance Court. Appeals against a decision of a local board go first to the national board and then, if necessary, to the court.

In addition to the local board, there are special bodies known as pension delegations and insurance committees. A pension delegation consists of two physicians appointed by the National Board of Health and Welfare, two persons appointed by the National Insurance Board, and two appointed by the county or municipal council. The chairman is the chairman of the local fund. An insurance committee consists of five to seven members, all appointed by the municipality. The pension committee is concerned with disability pensions, the insurance fund with basic pensions. The National Insurance Act provides that any board member, executive, or auditor may be charged with wilful injury or negligence.[4]

Counties and Municipalities

Some decentralization occurs from the national to the local levels. There are 24 county councils and administrative boards, and (as of 1974) 278 communes, or municipalities, sharing or dividing various public responsibilities.

While counties do not have the status of an intermediate level of government in the same sense as the Canadian provinces, they do serve to decentralize power in two ways: as units of national government administration, and as units for coordination of municipal interests. There are three kinds of bodies at the county level: regional boards acting as agents of the national boards just described; adminis-

Sweden: Relationship of Selected Administrative Boards to Political Structures

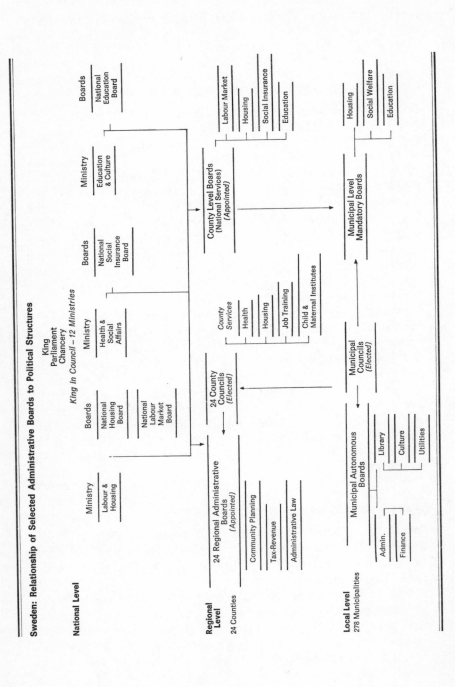

National Level

King
Parliament
Chancery
King in Council – 12 Ministries

Ministry	Boards	Ministry	Boards	Ministry	Boards
Labour & Housing	National Housing Board / National Labour Market Board	Health & Social Affairs	National Social Insurance Board	Education & Culture	National Education Board

Regional Level
24 Counties

24 Regional Administrative Boards
(Appointed)

Community Planning
Tax-Revenue
Administrative Law

24 County Councils
(Elected)

County Services
Health
Housing
Job Training
Child & Maternal Institutes

County Level Boards
(National Services)
(Appointed)

Labour Market
Housing
Social Insurance
Education

Local Level
278 Municipalities

Municipal Autonomous Boards

Admin.
Finance
Library
Culture
Utilities

Municipal Councils
(Elected)

Municipal Level Mandatory Boards

Housing
Social Welfare
Education

trative boards representing the national government in specified fields such as taxation, administrative law, child welfare, and community planning; and county councils, made up of representatives of local municipalities. The administrative boards are made up of representatives of management, labour, and county councils. They not only represent the national government at the regional level, but conversely are expected to convey local and regional interests to the national level.

The county councils, by contrast, are made up of representatives of the local municipalities in the counties. The councils are elected by direct vote, by proportional representation, at the same time as the national Riksdag elections. The most important function of the county councils (taking about 80 percent of the budget) is their administration of health care, including hospital services. They also provide services in vocational education, and are responsible for specialized institutions like nurseries, maternity homes, and correctional institutions. They are empowered to collect incometax for these purposes.

The county council has committees made up of elected council members, for health and medical services, social welfare (aid), legal aid, child care, vocational rehabilitation, dental care, and education (especially nursing education). These committees are paralleled by administrative departments responsible to them: county departments of medical services, social welfare, and education.

Municipalities are responsible for local utilities and for local administration of child welfare, public assistance, and basic education. They too, of course, have councils elected by proportional representation. Where the duties are mandatory, as in child welfare and education, that is, where the municipalities carry out national policy, they have no autonomy to make policy. They are independent only for local utilities, cultural and recreation services, and such matters.

Relatively few powers, it is seen, are controlled by local government as such, but representation of local and regional interests is assured. Otherwise, the diffusion of power occurs mainly in two ways: separation of political and administrative authority, and representation of owners, workers, and locally elected people on decentralized agencies of national boards.

CHAPTER THREE

Incomes and Jobs

THE LABOUR FORCE, WAGES, AND POLICY ISSUES

The Swedish population in 1971–72 was just over 8 million, of whom over 4 million were employees. About 300,000 persons are self-employed or owner-employers. An additional 1,170,000 were "inactive" income recipients;[1] that is to say, persons whose income did not come from employment. About 1.8 million were dependent children. The extent of coverage achieved is shown by the fact that a total of 6.3 million were adults eligible for social insurance benefits. Unemployment, by comparison with North America, was still low, at 2.7 percent in 1972, though higher than it had been in preceding years. In 1965 the rate was 1.2 and in 1970, 1.5. In absolute numbers, some 67,000 were registered unemployed in October 1972.

Income Distribution and Inequality

In Sweden it is common for both partners in a marriage to work, and family income is often taken as the true measure of financial security. But some categories of earners are obviously at a disadvantage and these groups become the focus of policy measures. Sweden is particularly concerned with female heads of families and with aging or aged people on single incomes. For a number of reasons unmarried men too have incomes considerably less than those of married men, but there is less concern over policy for them, possibly because a substantial number are very young, with no family responsibilities. Of unmarried men who did not declare taxable income in 1971, about 80 percent were under age 24.

A special Commission on Low Incomes was set up in 1966 to study the causes and distribution of low incomes. Their findings were much the same as those in other countries. Low incomes result from unemployment or from low pay when employed; age, sickness rates, and education are correlated with income. The most vulnerable groups are the disabled and elderly, and single mothers. In 1966, 15,000 kr. per annum was defined as the low-income line for households. Fifty-two percent of all people in the working age (20–66) had less than that amount. This figure is sharpened by looking at employment status. Of fully employed people, only 19 per cent received less than 15,000 kr., but of the partially employed, 65 percent, and of the unemployed, 97 per cent were below the poverty line. Age too contributed to poverty. Many of the unemployed under age 67 received early retirement or disability pensions. But pensions were inadequate. Of those over 67, on pension, 50–60 percent lived in households with gross incomes less than 10,000 kr. and 80 percent had less personal income than 10,000 kr.[2]

Income Differences by Marital Status, Sex, and Family Composition

In 1971, 46 percent of unmarried men had very low incomes of less than 10,000 kr. a year, compared with only 13 percent of married men. Probably this is because of the youth of many unmarried men. Just over 50 percent of unmarried men and about 65 percent of married men had between 10,000 and 40,000 kr., while in the affluent range, only 3.5 percent of unmarried men compared with 22 percent of married, had over 40,000 kr. a year.

Unmarried women, in contrast to men, were slightly better paid than married women, at least in terms of gross earnings. Of unmarried women, about 56 percent had under 10,000 kr., compared with about 63.5 percent of married women. About 41 percent of unmarried women and 35 percent of married women received from 10,000 to 40,000 kr., while only 2 percent of unmarried and 1.5 percent of married women earned over 40,000 kr.

The differences in income between married men and women are particularly obvious, but married women often work part-time, and since figures are reported as actual income earned rather than by

Table 3.1 **Incomes by Marital Status** (Percentage)

| | Men | | Women | |
	Married	Unmarried	Married	Unmarried
No declared income	3%	30%	27%	37%
Under 10,000 kr.	10	16	36.5	19
10–40,000 kr.	65	50.5	35	41
Over 40,000 kr.	22	3.5	1.5	2
	100%	100%	100%	100%

Source: Official Statistics of Sweden, *Income and Wealth Statistics, 1971*, Table 1.

rates of pay, it is hard to know whether the differences between sexes, or between unmarried and married women, is accounted for by the amount of time worked, rather than by sex, education, or other factors. The differences between unmarried men and women are a better indication of sex discrimination, but such differences are not as great as between married and unmarried of either sex.

The joint income of married couples almost invariably (and predictably) exceeds that of unmarried people, or of couples where only one works, so that in most families the satisfaction of family needs tends to be assured. It is so common for both to work that family income is reported in Swedish statistics as a base for policy.

About 95 percent of working couples earn more than 20,000 kr., over 60 percent earning more than 40,000 kr. The families in which both adults work represent about 73 percent of all families, so that about three quarters of Swedish families are at a relatively high in-

Table 3.2 **Income of Married Couples** (Percentage)

	Both working	One Working
Under 20,000 kr.	5.4%	13.6%
20,000–39,999	33.3	58.0
40,0000–59,999	40.1	19.5
Over 60,000	21.2	8.9
	100%	100%

Source: Official Statistics of Sweden, *Income and Wealth Statistics, 1971*, Table VI Stockholm, 1972.

come level. When only one member works, less than 30 percent earn more than 40,000 kr. But single-parent families receive special aid such as housing grants that help them maintain adequate standards.

The number of children in the family is not closely related to incomes, though there is a modest increase in income, as the number of children increases, of about 1,000 kr. per child per annum.

The differences in salaries relative to sex are very marked. The overall average income for working men in Stockholm in 1971 was 35,900 kr. while for women it was only about half as much, 18,500 kr. But these differences do not take account of time worked. National averages are shown in table 3.3.

Table 3.3 **All Income Earners, Average Income 1971**

	Male	Female
Employees	31,900 kr.	16,900 kr.
Employers/self-employed	28,300	16,900
Inactive	13,400	9,200

Source: *Income and Wealth Statistics, 1971*, Text-table 1, p. 11.

It is an interesting commentary on the status of work relationships in Sweden that "employers" nationally receive less on the average than employees. In Stockholm this relationship is reversed, though not sharply; the average for employers there was 36,700 kr. and for employees 30,000 kr.

The spread of incomes of men and women is best captured by quartile averages.

As noted before, married men earn more than unmarried, but unmarried women earn more than married. The range from the highest

Table 3.4 **Average Incomes in Lowest and Highest Quartiles, by Sex and Marital Status, 1971**

		Lowest Quartile	Highest Quartile
Men	Unmarried	10,800 kr.	28,100 kr.
	Married	20,300	39,200
Women	Unmarried	9,000	24,900
	Married	5,200	19,200

Source: *Income and Wealth Statistics, 1971*, from Text-table E.

quartile of 30,200 kr. for married men to the lowest quartile of 5,200 kr. for married women is considerable; but between sexes, within quartiles, the differences are not great.

Age and Incomes

If ages are also taken into account, the lowest average is found to be 7,000 kr., for the lowest quartile of unmarried men over the age of 67. The highest quartile for that age has an average of 20,000 kr.

The quartile averages (table 3.5) show the differences in income both by sex and among age-groups. The income spread for men is about double within each age-group; but the difficulties for women in the working years are reflected in even greater differences (related to time worked), both as between men and women and between the highest and lowest quartiles of women. The people of greatest concern here are the men and women age 67 and over. Their incomes are close to those under age 19, but the latter usually live in families so that their needs are not comparable with those of older people. Age is therefore a critical issue in incomes policy.

All men age 15 years and over numbered, in 1971, about 3,300,000. Of these, 455,000 were age 67 and more. Women too numbered 3,300,000, but almost 600,000 were 67 or more. Together, over a million people were of pension age, and their incomes were low. The income of pensioners ranged from a low of 7,400 kr. for the lowest quarter to a high of 18,600 kr. for the highest quarter of the men, and from 6,800 kr. to 15,300 kr. for women.

Thus Sweden has identified the elderly, handicapped persons, widows, and children as groups needing special attention in the development of income supports, as well as of employment programs

Table 3.5 **Average Incomes of Lowest and Highest Quartiles, by Age and Sex, 1971**

Age	Lowest Quartile		Highest Quartile	
	Men	Women	Men	Women
− 19	7,500 kr.	6,900 kr.	17,500 kr.	15,400 kr.
20–34	19,000 kr.	7,700 kr.	35,300 kr.	24,200 kr.
35–49	24,600 kr.	7,700 kr.	44,100 kr.	24,900 kr.
50–66	19,300 kr.	5,700 kr.	38,200 kr.	21,600 kr.
67 +	7,500 kr.	6,600 kr.	18,800 kr.	11,500 kr.

Source: *Income and Wealth Statistics, 1971*, Table 2.

Table 3.6 **Distribution of All Income Earners, by Level of Income** (Percentage)

Income Level	Percentage of Earners
Under 10,000 kr.	33.2%
10–20,000	21.2
20–30,000	21.3
30–40,000	14.6
40–60,000	7.0
Over 60,000	2.7

Source: *Income and Wealth Statistics, 1971*, Table 1.

for those able to use them. A lot of the legislation since 1966 has, in fact, been directed toward reducing inequalities of work and income for these groups.

Individual Earnings

If individual income is considered rather than family income, the general distribution remains about the same. A third of the incomes are below 10,000 kr., though the effect of this in standard of living is moderated by the fact that these are individual, not family incomes. The inadequacy of 10,000 kr. is indicated by the fact that average *take-home pay* (after taxes) in 1970 was about 1,825 kr. a month, over 17,000 kr. a year.[3]

From the point of view of earnings, therefore, while there is a range of five to six times in incomes from the lowest to the highest average, this in itself may not seem very great to Canadian eyes. The largest group of concern would seem to be the elderly, and pensioners have indeed received much attention.

Income by Type of Work

Variations that occur in income levels among economic sectors will be familiar in all modern societies. Not surprisingly, the lowest averages are in the category of the primary occupations of farming, forestry, fishing and hunting, and in the undefined "other" category, presumably in unskilled and short-term employment. More unusual is the fact that the highest incomes are in public services. The overall income range for men from the lowest to the highest quartile is about 1:7 and for women about 1:10, but median ranges are much less.

Table 3.7 **Incomes by Branch of Economy and Sex, 1971**
(Thousands of Kronor)

	Median Income		Lowest Quartile		Highest Quartile	
	Men	Women	Men	Women	Men	Women
Agriculture, forestry fishing	19.1	7.5	11.8	3.5	27.8	14.8
Mining, manu- facturing	28.6	16.2	21.3	9.1	36.9	23.8
Construction	27.9	14.4	20.0	6.2	36.4	24.0
Trade and catering	27.5	14.3	18.6	8.0	38.0	20.9
Transport and comunication	31.3	19.5	22.7	10.8	37.9	27.3
Public administra- tion services	35.3	16.2	23.7	7.8	50.7	26.0
Other	15.0	5.5	7.7	2.7	29.9	9.4
Total	28.8	15.5	20.2	7.8	37.9	24.4

Source: *Income and Wealth Statistics, 1971*, Table 15.

The numbers involved should also be recognized; fewer than 1.5 percent of male income-earners were in the "other" category and less
than 8 percent in agriculture, forestry, etc. Thus 90 percent of male
income-earners were in the higher-paid sectors, where the income
range is quite limited, from a lowest quartile of 18,600 kr. in trade
and catering, to a highest quartile of 50,700 kr. in public service, before taxes. Even fewer women (about 5 percent) are in the "other"
and "agriculture" categories. The wider ranges among women are
accounted for mainly by the numbers working part-time. The most
marked differences, as already observed, are between the sexes, but
the differences among economic sectors are remarkably small and
therefore do not constitute major policy problems. The social security
benefits based on income, therefore, will show relative uniformity
among economic sectors.

LABOUR MARKET POLICY

Social security in the limited sense is concerned with programs financed
by contributory insurance. Sweden's programs are much broader than

this, being concerned both with workers as contributors, and with non-contributors. The broader meaning of the term is used here in describing its programs.

The objectives of Swedish social policy, including manpower policy, are summarized by Alva Myrdal,[4] who identifies as those hardest hit by society, the unemployed, especially the long-term unemployed, those whose unemployment is related to geographic or regional factors, those who have experienced occupational shifts, new entrants to the labour force, those with physical or mental handicaps, those with poor education, and women. Policy, she argues, should be directed toward equalization of education, improved housing and residential amenities, with wide participation in planning of community resources, equality between sexes including improvement of opportunities for the sexes to share family and work responsibilities. She proposes generally much more extensive democracy in the work environment.

Manpower policies are closely interwoven with health, education, and welfare policies, and represent perhaps more sharply than any other area Swedish attitudes about the kind of society they want. Some of the rights of workers, and benefits, are assured by legislation, others by agreement at the level of the national organizations of employers and employees. Labour organizations (unions) work for policies collectively, not only for general benefits for their membership, but for special groups of people in the population (especially the elderly and handicapped) and for improvements in social policy affecting the whole population. Manpower policy is developed and effected in a tripartite fashion by public authorities: the National Labour Market Board and the municipalities, the Employers' Association, and the Confederation of Trade Unions and their member organizations. Industrial democracy is being developed and assured by mutual agreement and by law. It will be useful to consider some of the programs at close hand, integrated as they are with other social provisions.

Support to Industry

There are some general aids to industry, quite similar to Canadian programs of regional development and manpower training. Firms may obtain grants for locating in designated areas, on the understanding that they will provide permanent employment to workers there. Training grants are also paid, on the same understanding, to train regional workers. Additional special grants are paid to firms, also to subsidize wages in the initial three years in a new location. Also, firms are allowed to deposit money in a special fund, tax-free, and invest it for development purposes, subject to approval. None of these seem unusual to modern industrialized societies.

Job Placement

Procedures in the local placement offices are directed towards aiding the worker more than towards protecting the employer. An interesting system has been adopted of "self-serve" referrals whereby job applicants are informed of job openings and helped to make the choice and the application themselves, using employment-office telephones. The offices offer vocational guidance, including testing, and can pay the cost of the worker's travel to employment interviews. Generally, the employer is not required to use the employment service for hiring, or to notify it of vacancies, but other regulations may require supervision and sometimes enforcement of policy in the employer's practices. An example of policy to help older workers is that at least 25 percent of building workers on a construction contract must be over 50 years of age. If an employer does not observe such a regulation, the county labour board may require him to hire only their referrals until the condition is satisfied.

Vocational training is very extensive (about 120,000 people took training in 1971–72) and is operated jointly by the Labour Market Board and Education Board. The curriculum is developed jointly, the teaching and facilities are furnished largely by the Education Board, and financing of trainees carried by the Labour Market Board. The grants to trainees include *basic monthly allowances* of 665 kr. for general income to heads of families (615 kr. to others), *rent allowances* of at least 225 kr. or the actual current cost the recipient has to pay, *subsistence allowances* of 375 kr. to heads of families (225 kr. to others), *child allowances* of 125 kr. each, and *travel allowances*. The maximum combined grant in 1973 was 1700 kr. per month. The success rate of training is fairly high: 70 percent find jobs within three months after completion.

Removal grants may be made to the individual worker to cover the cost of moving to a new job for himself and his family. This includes the cost of looking for work; commuting for up to six months; a lump sum "start-up" grant up to 1500 kr. (or up to 2000 kr. plus 150 kr. per child in areas of high unemployment) to aid readjustment; a monthly grant up to one year if two houses have to be maintained, of 450 kr. plus 100 kr. per child; a seasonal relocation subsidy of 300 kr. a month. In addition, the state will guarantee to buy a house at standard rates if a man cannot sell when moving to a new job.

Job Stabilization

Assistance to firms as well as limitation of their freedom of action is also found in regard to discharge of numbers of workers, to ease unemployment during transition periods. Firms may be subsidized to help them over slack periods. There is a long-standing agreement between the Employer's Federation and the Labour Organization that employers will give *advance warning* to employment offices, of reduction of work affecting at least five workers, or closures. The period of warning varies with the number of workers affected, up to four months if at least a hundred workers are affected. Apart from subsidies, government contracts are also used to stabilize production by firms threatened with closure. The government may also guarantee the wages due to workers of a bankrupt firm, up to 7600 kr. per worker. Advance warning of layoffs also requires consultation with the worker and the union, including discussion of priorities for rehiring laid-off workers. Advance notice must also be given to workers who have been employed for twelve months in the past two years. The length of notice increases with age, from two months at age 25 to six months at age 45, or full pay.

Severance Pay

Another agreement between the Swedish Employers' Federation and unions covers *severance pay*, financed by an insurance plan, and designed especially to protect older workers. There are two levels of pay. An *A* rate is payable to men over 50 who lose their jobs as a result of production changes and who have worked mainly full time for ten years. This benefit is 100 kr. for each employment year. The *B* rate is payable to men under 62 who cannot get another job (including physical incapacity) or to men who are between 62 and 67. The benefit is cash up to 6000 kr.

Handicapped people are helped by work training in real work situations, and may take special adjustment courses. Grants or interest-free loans may be given to help them set up small businesses, up to 15,000 kr. and a further low-interest loan of 30,000 kr. Firms may be paid in-service training grants for handicapped workers, or grants to pay work assistants for the handicapped (for example, for blind persons).

The government subsidizes *special relief* work of various kinds, including so-called archive or white-collar work as well as manual labour and sheltered workshops. The work may be organized by the Labour Market Board directly, or by municipalities; in the latter case, the government pays 33 percent of the cost. At the beginning of 1972, over 32,000 people were employed in work of this kind. If laid off temporarily, the worker is entitled to full pay for any time over 14 days, and if dismissed for lack of work is entitled to the first option of rehiring. The county labour board can order an employer to rehire a worker who has been improperly dismissed.

These measure suggest that, increasingly, Swedish firms are viewed as social rather than private institutions. They are given financial aid to encourage success but, along with it, limitation of their decisions. Employment is the source of social wealth, and society takes the right both to ensure income through work, and to stabilize and ensure the production of wealth, without owning the machinery of production. At the same time, for those who cannot or should not work, blame is not attached, and benefits are so far as possible assured, either through contributory insurance programs or by noncontributory maintenance.

CHAPTER FOUR

Social Security Programs in Sweden

UNEMPLOYMENT INSURANCE

Coverage and Eligibility

Unemployment insurance has been managed traditionally by forty-four unemployment benefit societies, directed by trade unions under the supervision of the National Labour Market Board. While most insured people are union members, this is not an absolute condition of participation. There are about 2.5 million insured workers. A smaller proportion of the labour force is covered than in Canada. The usual conditions of eligibility prevail in Sweden, as in most countries. A claimant must be over 16 and under 67 years of age, must have contributed to a society for at least twelve months, five of which must be in the year preceding the claim. He must register for work and must not refuse suitable job offers, unemployment must be involuntary and not caused by a labour dispute in which the claimant is involved. In 1974 only about 2.6 million were covered, out of a labour force of 4 million, but this included about 80 percent of full-time workers. Those not covered included such people as part-time or elderly workers.

Contributions

Contributions to unemployment insurance are shared by employees and the state. Individual contributions are deducted at source, along with union dues. In all, employees' contributions amount to about

10 percent of the cost; 90 percent comes officially from the state, but of this about two-thirds is charged back to employers in taxes. The government subsidy varies considerably between funds, according to the type and number of beneficiaries.

Benefits

The unemployment benefit payable by the societies in 1971 was variable by categories between 18 and 60 kr. a day, dependent on wages and contributions, plus 2 kr. a day per dependent child. Coverage extended for 150 to 200 days depending on the society. In addition, even single uninsured persons were covered by a flat grant of 24 kr. a day, and couples 28 kr., plus 2 kr. per child, tax free. In 1974, along with similar major reforms in health insurance and pensions, unemployment benefits were made taxable, and were increased. Insurance benefits now may provide up to 91.7 percent of the individual's normal wage, up to a maximum of 130 kr. a day, well within the average wage range. Furthermore, the benefit period was increased from 150 to 300 days, and to 450 days for older workers. By these changes, unemployment insurance was placed on a par with other income both as to the amount and as to taxation.

Cash Labour Market Assistance

In 1974 a new and important program was introduced. Cutting into the principle by which contributions and benefits are related to past work, unemployment benefits were made available for uninsured workers, in the form of cash labour market assistance. This is a flat grant of 35 kr. a day to those who have worked at least five months in the past twelve. The duration of benefit varies with age: 150 days up to age 55, 300 days from age 55 to 60, and indefinite time between ages 60 and 67. This benefit too is taxable. Two-thirds of the cost of this program will be paid by employers, the balance coming from public funds.[1] This benefit is not just another form of social assistance. It is based on attachment to the labour market, and as such can be claimed as a right. The burden of cost is not put on the individual worker but is shared by the economy as a whole.

EMPLOYMENT INJURIES

Employment injury insurance is within the jurisdiction of the National Social Insurance Board, and is administered locally by the public insurance benefit societies along with sickness and pensions. It is financed by employer contributions, with a state subsidy. Benefits are quite simiar to, and are coordinated with, sick benefits and health care. Compensation is paid according to the degree of disability, and is based on an income limit of up to five times the "base" amount (that is, tied to cost of living). In 1974, the upper limit for calculation of benefit was 40,500 kr., an amount that compares well with average wages. The program includes invalidity annuities, and survivor annuities.

HEALTH INSURANCE

The Swedish health insurance program is divided into two major components: health care, and cash sick benefits.[2] Health care is available to the whole population, while cash sick pay is available to working people as a partial replacement of lost income, or on a voluntary basis to a spouse at home or other person not earning income, to help them meet costs incurred through illness. Cash sick pay is thus a very important means of ensuring income distribution during this most common cause of income loss.

Health Care, General Provisions

What is most striking about health care is its diversity of service, and the universality of coverage. It tries to ensure that cost will not stand in the way of adequate treatment, while at the same time, there is a charge against users who can afford to pay. Health care includes hospital care, out-patient treatment at hospitals and clinics, office or home calls, all diagnostic services, prescription drugs, referral to specialists, dental treatment, and travel costs connected with treatment. In 1970, Sweden instituted what was known as the "7-kronor reform"[3] which meant that the user charge, or cost of any single treatment at a clinic would be limited to 7 kr., and to 15 kr. for a home call. By 1974 that rate had inflated to 12 and 20 kr. respectively, but the principle holds, protecting those with major or prolonged illnesses. Other reduced rates apply to other services.

Health services themselves (hospitals, clinics, public health, etc.) are the responsibility of county councils. Under this authority, it is possible to have free home nursing both from the district nurse, and even, if necessary, to receive a grant to pay relatives or others to provide home nursing care. Industrial injuries and illnesses are treated in coordination with the general health program. During the first 90 days, medical care is paid by health insurance. Then it is picked up by other funds, including one known as Employees' Liability. If long-term care is needed by an injured worker, he may receive a grant of 5 kr. a day in addition to other cash benefits.

Coverage

All Swedish citizens and registered noncitizens are covered for health care. Sickness benefits, however, are available only for compulsory contributors or spouses, or for those persons who make voluntary contributions. This excludes pensioners, who are covered automatically for health care. As of 1971, the total population was insured; there were over 6,300,000 insured members of 26 public insurance funds in the country, and their dependent children numbered about 1,800,000. Of the total population, 4,840,000 adults were covered for sickness cash benefit. About 970,000 were covered voluntarily for basic income, and approximately 3,918,000 odd had coverage under one of the higher, supplementary categories.[4] Of all those covered by health insurance, 76.7 percent were covered for the basic sick cash benefit, 62.1 percent had further supplementary benefits, and 19.7 percent were covered by disability or old age pensions. The significance of cash sickness benefits is obvious, as an instrument to avoid the disastrous inequalities resulting from loss of wages.

Contributions

Finances for the health insurance and sick benefit programs are derived from employees' contributions, employers, and the state. As of 1974, employees pay a fixed portion of 300 kr. a year, and a variable amount based on income. This combined employee contribution averages about 650 kr. a year and covers about one quarter of the cost. Employers pay 3.8 percent of the employees' wage up to an upper limit of insurable income, of 7.5 times a base amount. The base amount is an estimated national minimum income that is used in calculating most insurance benefits, and is adjusted frequently with the cost-of-living index. By setting a maximum of 7.5 as an upper limit for insurance purposes, Sweden recognizes and accepts an income spread of 7.5:1. At mid-1974, the base amount was 8400 kr. The state contributes about 50 percent of the cost of health services, maternity, and child supplements, and 20 percent of the cost of voluntary cash benefits.

Almost all (eleven-twelfths) of the employees' contributions are applied to the cost of health care, as is a third of the employer's contribution. The balances go to provide cash sick benefits. Spouses (either husbands or wives) and students may take out voluntary sick benefit insurance and increase family benefits thereby. People without taxable income need not contribute at all to health care.

Benefits

In summary, specific *health care benefits* are extensive:

Hospital: all costs free; no time limit except for pensioners

Physician's fees: refund beyond 12 kr. per clinic visit
      20 kr. per home visit

Travel: all costs over 6 kr. for patient and escort to hospital or clinic

Prescriptions: 50 percent of costs from 5 kr. to 25 kr.
      100 percent of costs over 25 kr.
      Maximum charge to patient 15 kr.

Dental Care: Children age 6–16 free
      Others, 50 percent of costs to 1000 kr.
      75 percent of costs over 1000 kr.

Industrial Injuries: Health and hospital care as above
      Dental care, glasses, orthopaedic service free
      After 90 days, all costs free

Home Care: District nurse visits free
      Home nursing grants to relatives or friends

V.D., T.B., Addiction: Free treatment

Cash Sick Benefit

Sick benefit before 1974 was paid according to income-related categories, including voluntary insurance for spouses at home, that provided a fixed amount (plus dependents' supplement) in each category. Since 1974 the program has been changed radically. The basic cash benefit for spouses, of 6 kr. a day, has been raised to 8 kr., tax free. The former child supplement that was used to provide for families was abolished, and workers' benefits were fixed at 90 percent of gross wage, up to 7.5 times the base amount, and were made taxable. The maximum insurable salary in mid-1974 was about 63,000 kr. a year, so that cash benefit could be as much as 56,700 kr. Under the old system, benefits of 6 kr. a day at the bottom of the income scale could be 100 percent of earnings, but they dropped rather steeply as income rose, to about 50 percent at the top cut-off point. However, the old benefits were not taxable. Because of the high tax rate at top levels, the new system may not result in much change in the relative scale of benefits at the top, though it might be more advantageous at middle levels. More important, the net benefits received will be almost equal to normal take-home pay.

Sick cash benefits have been widely used. In 1971, benefits were issued in 5,475,000 cases. The rate of use varies with age. For example, of the age group 16–19, 5.2 percent of persons registered drew benefits, while in the 60–66 age group the rate was 13.1 percent.[5] For all ages, the average number of days sick pay per registered insured person was 20.4, and the number of days per sick beneficiary was 39.9. The use of sick benefit also varied with the level of income (and contribution). While relatively high use occurred at the basic rate of 6 kr. a day, covering persons without income (long-term unemployed, housewives, etc.), it dropped at the level of very low-wage workers (whose benefits were from 7–12 kr. a day). It was highest at the middle wage level (benefits of 25–34 kr. a day), and was lowest at the top income levels of over 40 kr. a day.[6] It may be supposed that this does not mean that low-wage people were less often sick than middle-wage workers, but that they could not afford to stay away from work at the rate of compensation paid in 1971. The increase of benefit to 90 percent of wage may change rates of use.

Supplementary Benefits

In addition to compulsory sick benefit insurance for employees, there is a voluntary system providing supplementary benefits in several categories from 1 to 9 kr. a day. About half of those subscribing chose the top level coverage in 1971. The voluntary system allowed a choice of four waiting periods: none, 3 days, 33 days, and 93 days. Contributions are, of course, related to this choice. The great majority chose either no wait or the 3-day wait, because the contribution rates were not substantially greater than for the longer waiting periods. Sick pay has in principle no time limit, except in the case of people of pensionable age (67) where there is a limit of six months, after which the pension becomes operable.

Maternity Pay/Parent Pay

Another very important aspect of sick pay has been maternity coverage. To 1974, there was a lump sum benefit of 1080 kr. plus sick benefit for a total of 6 months (subject to an earnings limitation) covering the period before and after confinement. In 1971, there were about 70,000 beneficiaries, of whom 72.4 percent took the full 6-month benefit. However, another of the 1974 amendments replaced maternity benefit with an even broader program of parent benefits. Under this amendment, while the lump sum payment of 1080 kr. continues to the mother, parent benefit is payable to either parent. Payment is set at a minimum of 25 kr. a day for 6 months, or higher for insured parents according to salary, at the same rates as sick pay. Moreover, either the father or the mother may receive parents' benefits for 10 days a year to stay at home to look after a sick child up to age 10. This benefit too is taxable and pensionable. This is a major step in the direction of recognition that many mothers work, and of equal rights and responsibilities of parents for children.

PENSIONS

There are several kinds of benefits under the general heading of "pensions." The three major types are old-age, disability, and family or survivor pensions. Each of these is provided in two main categories of "national" and "supplementary." The national program is *non-contributory* (except through income tax) and therefore universal in coverage. It provides flat-rate benefits regardless of previous work. At the risk of confusion, there are also what are called supplements to the national program, for dependents.

The supplementary program by comparison is *contributory*, with benefits varying with contributions. Contributions are not made by individuals, however, but entirely by the state and by heavy charges to employers, who, in 1974, paid 10.5 percent of payroll for this program. The important principle is accepted here, that provision for old age, death, or disablement is not the responsibility of the individual, but of the state, and of society as a whole. Nevertheless, the contributory superannuation program is work-related.

Benefits

Old Age. The age of retirement varies among countries according to tradition, and to influences such as the labour market. When unemployment rates are high, pressures may mount for reduction of the retirement age by political decision, but since such decisions are almost irreversible, and are costly, they do not happen fast. In Sweden the age of retirement is 67. Old age pension may be drawn as early as age 63, but then the benefit is reduced by 0.6 percent for every month under 67. Retirement may also be postponed to as late as age 70, and the benefit then increases by 0.6 percent for every month over age 67.

All pensions (like health insurance) are calculated from the base amount or standard income that is indexed to the cost of living. In 1969 that base amount was 6000 kr. per annum, but in mid-1974 was at 8,400 kr. A full old-age national or basic pension is 90 percent of the base amount for single persons and 140 percent for pensioned couples. This is not a large amount of money, as indicated in the analysis of incomes, above. There is, in addition, a general supplement designed progressively to increase the effect of the base, that will, by 1978, provide an additional amount of 30 percent of the base. This general supplement is available for all pensions.

This benefit by itself would not be sufficient to keep the pensioner out of poverty, but there are several supplements to the national old age pension and disability pensions: first, a wife's supplement is available on means test for the wife of an old age pensioner if she is at least 60 years old but not yet herself a pensioner. In effect, this supplement will provide an income for a pensioner with a younger wife that will be the same as for a couple on pension, including the general supplement. Second, there is a child supplement amounting to 25 percent of the base amount per child. Third, there is a means-tested municipal housing supplement that varies with the municipality in its conditions and value.

The additional work-based supplementary pension or superannuation scheme (known as ATP) is payable in addition to the national basic pension. These pensions are calculated by a formula of annual pension points that are derived by dividing pensionable income earned in one year (the amount between the base amount and 7.5 times the base) by the base amount. This calculation takes account of changing values, since the pension points are expressed in terms of values each year. The cash amount of the pension is established by taking the average number of pension points earned over the worker's fifteen best years and multiplying that average by the base amount in effect at retirement, bringing it up to current value. A full pension requires thirty years' contribution, but lesser amounts may be earned down to as little as three years' contributions. A full ATP is 60 percent of average pension-carrying income during the previous years, and is reduced by one-thirtieth for every year less than thirty. This pension is indexed to the cost of living by recalculating it whenever the base amount rises. The whole system provides a safeguard against inflation both before and after retirement. The combined ATP and national pension, with supplements, provides an income reasonably close to the average the person received from wages.

Disability. Disability or "early retirement" pensions are payable when the person's work capacity is reduced by at least one-half, and is payable between the ages of 16 and 67 (at the latter age, it is replaced by old-age pension). These are non-contributory, national pensions, and the full benefit is, like old age pension, 90 percent of the base amount. Lesser benefits are proportionate to the degree of disability between one-half and full.

In addition to the national permanent disability or early retirement program, there is a temporary disability or sickness benefit for periods over one year but less than permanent. The conditions and benefits are the same as for the usual disability program. There are also supplementary programs calculated just as in the supplementary old age programs. There is the *general supplement* to the basic pension, then a wage-related *contributory supplementary* program like the old age supplementary pension, but using a system of "assumed" pension points so that a disabled person's eligibility is calculated as if he had earned points. There is a *supplementary disablement "allowance"* of 2370 kr. a year for old age or "early retirement" pensioners who are blind or so disabled as to need extra care. There is a *"disablement compensation"* of 4740 kr. a year for blind or disabled persons who are gainfully occupied or studying but not receiving a pension. There is a "care allowance" equal to a full disability pension, for the parent of a disabled child requiring long-term special care. Finally, there are "life annuities" for persons injured in industrial accidents. The amount of annuity is related to wage levels and to the degree of disablement if that exceeds 10 percent of earning capacity. The supplements described above for old age pensioners, for wives, children, and municipal housing, are also available for disability pensioners.

Family Pensions (Survivors'). Family pensions distinct from wives' and children's supplements to pensioners, are in effect survivors' pensions, and include provision for widows and orphans. Here again there is the basic national pension provision. A widow's pension is payable to any widow over 36 years old who was married at least five years before the man's death. If she was at least 50 at the time of death, she will receive his full benefit, that is 90 percent of the base amount. This is reduced by one-fifteenth for every year under 50, except that if she has a child under 16 there is no deduction. A child will receive 25 percent of the base amount, or 35 percent if both parents are dead.

Again, as with old age and disability pensions, there is a supplementary provision based on contributions for widows and orphans. If there are no children under 18 years of age, the widow receives a supplement of 40 percent of the pension (whether it was an old-age or disability pension) and if there were children, the supplement to the widow is increased by 15 percent for each child. If there are no parents, a child receives, as of 1974, 60 percent of the father's pension, with the addition of 10 percent for each subsequent child.

In summary, the pension program provides a national noncontributory assurance of basic income (indexed to living costs) to pensioners, disabled persons, blind persons, widows and orphans, and in addition contributory supplements to each of these kinds of beneficiaries. Health care is assured under the National Health plan, and housing is assured under a variety of housing programs including municipal supplements. Complete as appears the coverage of these programs, the relative inadequacy of *basic* pensions, even with the cost-of-living supplements, is shown in the figures for 1972, as compared with average wages discussed earlier.

Table 4.1 Average Basic Pensions Including Supplements, 1972

Old age and disability pensions	7446 kr. per year
Wives' supplements	4526
Child pension (1 parent)	1825
Disability allowance	4380

Source: Official Statistics of Sweden, *National Insurance, 1971*, Table 12.14.

The amount of supplementary pensions also remains low relative to wage levels. The average supplement for old age male pensioners in 1971 was 2772 kr. and for women 1638 kr. For full disability pensions it was higher: 5756 kr. for men and 3198 kr. for women, and for temporary disability even more (8046 kr. for men, 6653 kr. for women). Widow's pension was again low, at 2823 kr. The average municipal housing supplement to old age pensioners was 1179 kr., and to disability pensioners 1276 kr., in 1971. However, when all these are added to the basic pension, and to health services, the total represents a liveable income, especially for couples. Certainly, total benefits are well above the "base amount" and approach the lower end of the modal range of wages.

Coverage. The total number of people receiving national basic pensions in January 1971 was about 1,400,000, of whom 970,000 were old age pensioners (430,000 men and 540,000 women) and 183,000 disability pensioners. The rest received temporary disability pensions, widows' or children's pensions. General pension supplement was paid to 825,000 of the old age pensioners, and municipal housing supplement to 520,000. Child supplement was paid to only 1400, and disability supplement to 1900. The supplements to disability pensioners and widows were in similar proportion except that disability pensioners, having more children, had more child supplements, and they not unnaturally had more disability supplements.

Supplementary (contributory) pensions were received in January 1971 by 466,800 people of whom over 261,000 were old age pensioners (203,000 men and 58,000 women).

Table 4.2 **Pension Recipients, 1971**

	National Pensions	Supplementary Pensions	
Old age (Men 429,919) (Women 538,674)	968,593	261,766 (Men 203,294) (Women 58,472)	
Disability	183,576	75,433	
Temporary disability	18,898	17,284	
Disability allowance	11,355		
Wife's supplement	59,549		
Widows' pension	104,340	80,108	
Child pension	33,949	32,209	
Transitional	21		
	1,390,281	466,800	

Source: Official Statistics of Sweden, *National Insurance, 1971*, Tables 12.1, 12.14.

It is noted that while women outnumbered men in the national pension program, three times as many men as women received supplementary pensions based on contributions. Also striking is the fact that of almost a million national old age pensioners, only a little over a quarter shared in the supplementary program (less than half the men and little more than one-tenth of the women). Of disability pensioners, less than half received supplementary pensions. The national program is obviously very important as a way to provide basic income, and its inadequacy becomes all the more significant. It is understood, also, that women would not have earned supplementary pensions, since so many do not work, either full-time or for long periods. But it is also clear that the supplementary program does not yet meet the need. It may be that as newer policies take effect (such as sick pay being available for either parent during maternity leave and being considered part of pensionable earnings), and as more women work, the numbers of women receiving adequate supplementary pensions will increase. It is surprising and disturbing to see how relatively few men earn any supplement; presumably due to the fact that the supplementary program was not established until 1960, so that it has not yet taken full effect.

OTHER SOCIAL BENEFITS

Several important kinds of benefit are available on a national scale that are not included in the social insurance programs, but that go to make up the total package of social provisions.

Housing

Housing has been an object of special attention and support in Sweden. Various kinds of subsidies and incentives are available. *State loans* are made available, through county housing boards, to cover part of mortgages. Tenant-owner associations can get 25 percent of the value of the building, and nonprofit building societies 30 percent. Twenty percent is available to owner-occupiers. Twenty percent must come from a bank. *Improvement loans* are available to private owners up to 90 percent of the cost, either as interest-free grants (up to 12,000 kr.) or as low-rate loans at 4 percent, for the balance. Local authorities and nonprofit societies can get interest-free loans for 100 percent of the cost of renovation.

Tax-free *state rent allowances* are paid to families with children, based on the number of children, size of income, and size of dwelling, but the income ceiling is set quiet high, so that a family with five children could receive aid (1974) even with an income of 37,000 kr. (well above average). The allowance amounts to 75 kr. a month per child, up to an income of 23,000 kr., declining at higher levels of income. Since the allowances increase with unit size, it pays families to occupy suitably large houses. A family with five children could get as much as 4500 kr. per year, which could be between 10 and 20 percent of the average family's annual income.

In addition to state allowances, there are *municipal rent allowances*, to which the national government contributes, for large low-income families and all three types of pensioners. Allowances vary among municipalities. Generally, the emphasis is on ensuring good quality housing, and the allowances rise as adequate house quality (space and equipment) improves. Depending on the rent and number of children, the allowance may be up to about a quarter of the rent. Subject to a rent ceiling, the general rule is a grant of 80 percent of any rent beyond 300 kr. for a single-parent family or beyond 400 kr. for a two-parent family. In the case of pensioners, the allowance, which is tax-free, varies with income alone. At noted earlier, over half the country's pensioners received a municipal housing allowance.

Municipalities are primarily responsible for housing planning. They operate public utility companies renting blocks of flats, in competition with private enterprise. There is a Rent Act governing rent levels, with county rent tribunals. There are, as well, tenant associations that assist and represent tenants in disputes. Rent is such a public affair that it can be paid in to a post office rather than to the landlord, even in the case of private ownership. "Security of tenure" is achieved by a tenant after nine months' occupancy in good standing. This means he has a prior claim on renewal of the lease.

In addition to the public housing companies, there are *tenant-owner associations*, often set up as cooperatives, that are in effect condominiums. Members share the taxes and other building costs. In 1970, about 35 percent of all housing units in Sweden were owned by public authorities or cooperative societies, and the proportion is growing. In 1971, 60 percent of new housing was built for these authorities. Nonrepayable home improvement loans at low interest act, in effect, as grants for low-income families and pensioners.

Home furnishings loans are also available at low interest, subject to an income ceiling of 35,000 kr. In 1971, 518,667 households received national and/or municipal allowances in addition to the municipal allowances for pensioners mentioned above.

Family Allowances

Family allowances are universally available for all children up to age 16, at a rate (1974) of 1,320 kr. a year. In addition, there is an unusual program of "maintenance allowances" that are paid to children of separated parents. This amounts to 40 percent of the social insurance "base amount," and assures maintenance of a child even when parents are neglectful. Home helps are available for pensioners (aged or disabled) who need help in the home, for families where a parent is ill, or where parents work but a child is ill. These helpers are subsidized by municipalities, with the support of state grants in the amount of 35 percent of the cost. Users are charged according to their ability to pay. About 85,000 "home helps" were employed in 1973, many of them relatives of the families in need. The program thus acts as another form of subsidy in the event of illness.

Social Assistance

Social assistance is a municipal responsibility, aid being conditional on need. It is a small program, but seems to generate criticism since it is unrelated to work or contributions.

In 1972 there were over 250,000 families (over half a million people) for whom assistance was given. However, authorities say the total cost of such aid (about 496 million kr. in 1972) is a very small percentage of all social costs, and it is demonstrated that little assistance goes to employable people. Most is used as supplements to other programs.

Fringe Benefits

Employers in Sweden are charged directly for contributions to the major statutory insurance programs, as discussed above. In addition to those, some major benefits are negotiated for employees by the Swedish Employers' Confederation and the Labour Organization for large numbers of both blue and white-collar workers. Several items resulted in increased charges to employers in 1974, with changes in government policy. The negotiated benefits have been used to complement statutory programs, and because they are legally binding on so many employers, they have the effect of law. Contributions come entirely from employers. Premiums for statutory and voluntary benefits for 1974 cost employers large percentages of annual wages (see table 4.3).

Of the above, five programs are statutory: national pensions, health insurance, industrial injuries insurance, unemployment insurance, and vacation pay. Complementary programs for sick pay and pensions have been available for salaried workers for many years, but it was only in the seventies that these benefits were acquired for wage workers—complementary sick pay from 1972 and pension from 1973. These programs are handled by nonprofit "labour market insurance companies" set up for the purpose by the Employers' Confederation and the Labour Organization. In the case of workers' sick pay, the insurance company has contracted with the cooperative movement's

Table 4.3 **Statutory and Negotiated Benefits as Percentage of Wages and Salaries, 1974**

	Wage Workers	Salaried Workers
National Supplementary pensions	8.0	8.0
National Health Insurance	3.8	3.5
Industrial Injuries Insurance	0.4	0.3
Unemployment Insurance	0.4	0.4
General basic pension	3.3	3.0
Group life insurance	0.4	0.3
Complementary pension	2.0	8.6
Complementary health insurance	1.1	0.6
Severance pay	0.2	0.5
Vacation pay	8.1	8.2
General payroll tax	4.0	4.0
Total	31.7	37.3

Source: Swedish Employers' Confederation, *Non-Wage Labour Costs in Sweden, 1974*, Stockholm, 1975. Mimeo.

insurance company to administer the services, and pensions have been assigned for administration to the Swedish Staff Pension Society which has handled the salaried workers' programs.

The major difference between blue- and white-collar workers is in the percentage of contributions to complementary pensions. In both cases, a major purpose of the complementary pension program is to provide retirement income or disability pension from age 65, to fill in the gap to age 67 when the national pensions are payable. In addition, in the case of salaried workers, the complementary amount increases the pension by raising the limit of contributions on pensionable income from the statutory 7.5 times the "base amount" to 15 times, thus providing much higher retirement incomes for high-paid staff. The same higher benefits are available for widows of salaried employees. Wage workers' benefits are much lower. The benefits before age 67 are very like the amounts provided by the national scheme at age 67, and after age 67 increase those of the national scheme by 10 percent of the workers' pensionable wages.

The major aim of complementary sickness insurance was to increase to about 90 percent of wages the sick pay received under the national plan. Benefits were thus tied to the sick pay categories previously used as a basis for calculating benefits. Since 1974 with the increase in benefits to 90 percent of wages, this purpose has been satisfied, and changes in both contributions and benefits will be required.

Beyond these major programs, companies offer various other benefits, such as subsidized meals at work, travel costs, work clothes, recreation facilities, and health care. However, these are not included in the agreements concluded by the major representatives of employers and workers, and there is no general pattern of benefits.

CONCLUSION

The intention of Swedish social policy is clear: to do everything possible to involve as many people as possible in gainful work, but at the same time to provide for contingencies of loss of work income by a series of programs designed to reduce the gap between wages and nonwage incomes. Sickness benefits and unemployment insurance now approach full wages. However, the gap remains large for vulnerable groups: old people, the disabled or handicapped, widows and children. How large the gap is, or how rapidly it is being closed, is a matter of detailed examination by various Swedish authorities. There is a lot of catching up to do, partly by raising the basic benefits, partly by ensuring that they do not slip back with increases in the cost of living. This is to be done by making benefits as generous as possible, tying them to earned income during periods of contribution, but then submitting them to normal income-tax rates, by which means net incomes are kept within a limited range.

Some Swedish authorities are not greatly enamoured of the idea of the guaranteed annual income, obviously not because they disagree with the principle of equalization, but to the contrary. They think a guaranteed income may cover up a multitude of inequities or failures of service for those who need special attention. Therefore Swedish researchers investigate and identify the needs of various populations, and take special steps to meet those needs.

Sweden has paid great attention to the issues of maximization of resources, and equalization of their distribution, but less to the allocation of roles and powers. They have so far accepted the capitalist structure as the most efficient base for creation of resources, and have used traditional centralized political structures for policy changes, relying on the bargaining power and political unity of unions to create a political balance with employers and to effect a better distribution of resources to nonunion as well as union people.

Sweden has not been greatly concerned with grass-roots democracy,

American style, probably because the government is seen by many as the agent of the people, rather than as the representative of special interests. Local structures have not involved large numbers of people; there seems to have been more concern with bureaucratic efficiency and accountability, and with assurance that policy-making was accessible to the representatives of the major unions than with widespread distribution of political roles. However, there are indications that union members themselves are uneasy with a focus on efficiency alone, and that increased participation in both industrial management and political affairs will be demanded in future.[7] For example, a Commission on Social Welfare, reporting in 1964,[8] recommended the clear assignment of social welfare duties to the municipal level, on the principle that more people should be involved in solving mutual problems and that the engagement of more people could only occur at the local level. This principle of the development and extension of political roles to a local community base should help to equalize both resources and powers.

Part 3

Yugoslavia

CHAPTER FIVE

The Socialist Federal Republic of Yugoslavia

Modern Yugoslavia was born in 1943 by caesarean section, as it were, through a heroic patriotic defence against fascist invaders that became at the same time a revolution against the monarchy. For millenia, this land of almost impenetrable mountains has been repeatedly invaded, dismembered, and occupied by a series of foreign conquerors in whose way it stood: Greeks, Romans, Turks, Venetians, Austrians, Germans, Italians. It encompasses the remnants of many peoples and their cultures, whose outlook is understandably regional and defensive. It could scarcely avoid being a federal state, composed as it is of six fiercely independent nations: Slovenia, Croatia, Bosnia-Hercegovina, Serbia, Montenegro, and Macedonia. Serbia, furthermore, contains two autonomous provinces of Kosova and Vojvodina, which both contain large minority populations originating in neighbouring countries of Albania, Hungary, and Bulgaria. The country's religions are mixed: one of the first areas to be Christianized, but with a long Muslim occupation, it is now officially atheist. There are three separate languages and two scripts among its twenty million people.

The country is unevenly endowed physically and historically, with resulting inequalities among the republics in the size and productive capacities of their populations. Some have good arable land, some have not; some have a long coastline, some have not. The population varies. The largest republic, Serbia, had in 1971 about eight and a half million people. Croatia had less than 4,500,000, Bosnia-Hercegovina about 3,700,000, Macedonia and Slovenia had each about 1,700,000, and Montenegro only 500,000.

The wealth of the republics is not directly related to their size. The highest standards of living are enjoyed in Slovenia, which was at one time part of the Austro Hungarian Empire. The poorest is Macedonia, isolated, and with few resources.

The country is committed to decentralization and self-management. This being so, and given the differences of resources, it is natural that there are rather wide ranges of incomes, of work opportunities, and of social benefits. While attention will be given in the following chapters to a general outline of social security for the country as a whole, it was considered preferable to concentrate more detailed examination on the programs of Slovenia. This is the most affluent and in some ways therefore the most optimistic expression of Yugoslav social security programs, but is still representative of the policies of the whole country.

MAJOR STRUCTURES AND PROCESSES OF GOVERNMENT

During its short life as a federated republic, (since 1943), Yugoslavia has been through a series of constitutions and stages of political goals that have reflected her internal history, geopolitical location and political parentage. The Communist Party was the political force that created the nation and brought it successfully out of war, but the lessons of Stalin, Hungary, and Czechoslovakia have created a deep revulsion against centralist control, especially by Moscow.

Several sets of conflicting necessities have faced the leaders. They were Communists, but found themselves more friendly to and less fearful of the west than the east. They needed national economic and social growth, but could not and would not enforce it by political centralism. They believed in socialist democracy and industrialization, though many of the people were technically unskilled peasants who were accustomed to protecting their own individual holdings against all comers.

In their efforts to deal with those and other dilemmas, the leadership has taken the people through several major changes, each of which, as it secured one aspect, risked another. The first position after the war was identification with the Comintern as a Soviet-style centralist state. After that, about 1950, the next stage was serious rupture with Moscow and adoption of decentralized "self-management" combined with a market approach to economic management that led to increasing signs of personal opportunism and social inequality. But this policy also tended to create ideological and practical tensions by separating political authority from economic and social activities.

THE NEW CONSTITUTION

In January 1974, a new constitution was adopted. It is clearly influenced by, and designed to cope with, the major dilemmas. It is complex, detailed, and untried. Perhaps its main difficulty is that it is a document dealing with the present rather than one for all times. It uses terms and proposes structures that will change. No doubt as it shakes down, its true effects will emerge and new changes will be made. Meanwhile its intent seems positive. In brief, it seeks two objectives: to establish a principle of wide participation that places self-management at the top of political values, that is, making policy from the bottom up rather than from the top down; and to merge political, social, and economic planning by creating political structures that require the interdependence of these interests.

The 1974 Constitution identifies three levels of government and assigns areas of responsibility to each: the Federal Republic, the Republic, and the Commune. These are called "socio-political communities." It also identifies a fourth level, the local community or neighbourhood, similar to a ward, which has organized certain local services within the Commune and is an electoral base for political representation, but has no governing power. The Commune is the basic governing body for which all citizens vote in general elections. Representation to the Republic and Federal assemblies is by election from Commune assemblies.

A second set of structures are "organizations of associated labour." These are all those formally constituted organizations or enterprises in which work is done, including "economic" or goods production, public services, and private ventures. When semi-independent divisions of these organizations exist (as in product-differentiated industries) they are called "basic organizations of associated labour." These organizations are in effect the economic backbone of society. The workers make economic decisions and pay the bills.

A third type of social institution is "communities of interest." These are all those activities that provide common services in society. They are identified as including at least health, education, social welfare, pensions and social security, housing, scientific activities, culture, and public utilities such as power, water, and transport. These "communities" may again be subdivided. For example, the community of social

Yugoslavia: Structure of Government

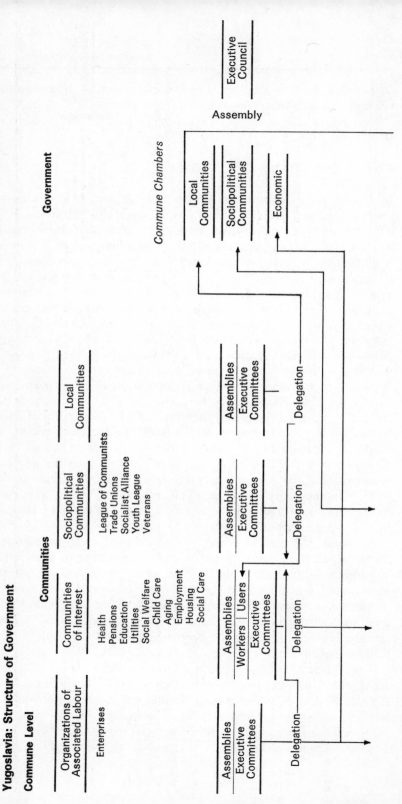

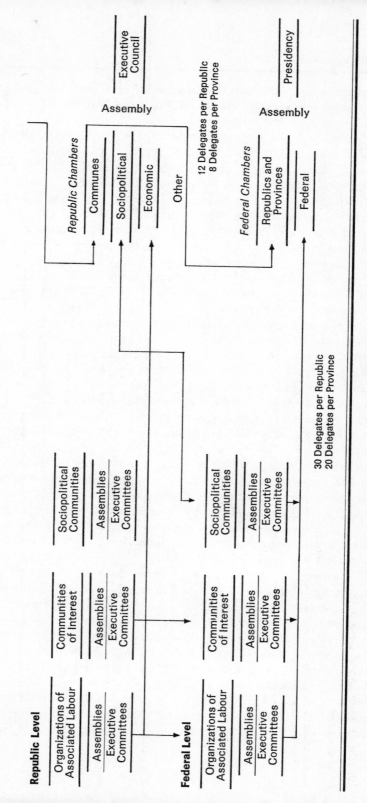

welfare is subdivided into communities for child care, the aged, housing, employment, and "social care," or social services. These groups include most of the professionals.

A fourth kind of organization identified as having certain significant rights and duties in the constitution, are the "socio-political organizations." They are the Communist Party (its significant title is The League of Communists of Yugoslavia), the Socialist Alliance of the Working People of Yugoslavia, the Federation of Trade Unions, the Youth League, and the War Veterans' Federation. Of these, the Communist Party is described as the "vanguard" of political thought and action. It consists of a relatively small number of people, who are not given any specific status, but whose leadership responsibility is identified. The duty of political organizations is to help define political objectives and economic objectives by leading in discussion whenever opportunity arises.

Organizations of associated labour, communities of interest, and socio-political organizations exist at commune, republic, and federal levels, parallel to the three formal government levels, and are linked to governments at three levels by systems of delegation and assemblies. This is not so that formal authority can be delegated to them by higher levels of government, but so that delegates can carry instructions to the three levels of government from the constituent parts.

All economic, social, and political organizations must have two main structures: assemblies, and executive councils. The assembly is the membership as a whole, in which final authority for the operation of the organization resides. The executive council and officers are elected by the assembly, for management of the organization. In addition, delegates are elected by all working and interest organizations for the purpose of representing the organization in parallel bodies, especially in the public service "communities of interest," and in government, or socio-political assemblies.

The delegates of all basic work organizations meet in a delegates' conference at the level of the commune, that in turn elects delegates in the number called for, to the assemblies of the communities of interest and to the commune assembly. The purpose of this system is to provide interlocking networks, and so to stimulate the interest and participation of working people in and through their work relationships in social and political issues. It is hoped to counteract a tendency toward professionalization of politics and equally to counteract professional domination of services. The proposal is to keep all working people aware of the importance of self-management and self-determination in all matters affecting them, generally, to broaden the popular base of political involvement. Delegates are supposed to carry discussions back to the assemblies of their work organizations.

Another feature of the delegate system designed to widen political participation is that, given the very wide range of subjects to be discussed, seats on various bodies are held by different people at different times, depending on the agenda, so that those with special interest and competence may represent their organization as occasion warrants. Thus each work organization may elect one delegate to several communities of interest or one to each community, but when one of the communities sends its delegates to the commune assembly or to meet other communities of interest, to debate specialized subjects, it will choose those with special interest or competence. Responsibility may thus be more widely shared.

The Commune has at least three chambers: the economic chamber, representing work organizations and special interest communities; the chamber of local communities, representing all citizens on a geographic or residential base, working or not; and the chamber of socio-political organizations. Since most working people (97 percent in Slovenia) are organized in unions, and workers are all automatically members of the Socialist Alliance, they are entitled to elect representatives to the socio-political chamber of the commune. Since all residents can also vote in a local community, this gives them a second vote, this time for the chamber of local communities. And all working people can also vote for delegates to the economic chamber of work organizations. Each chamber may propose laws on any subject, but before a law is passed it must be discussed and approved by the others. Most proposals will originate with work organizations, communities, or socio-political organizations. Thus, for example, decisions on budgets for education will be proposed by the community for education and are passed finally by the assembly chambers, but only after opportunity for discussion on costs and policy at the level of work organizations, unions, and other communities of interest in the commune. For purposes of representing their own fields, the communities of interest become members (can send a delegate) to the assembly of the Commune and, through the republic level of the community, to the Assembly of the Republic.

Communities of Interest

The communities of interest, unlike economic organizations where the Assembly consists of all workers, have double chambers representing consumers, as well as producers or workers in the service

Yugoslavia: Relationship of Commune Structures

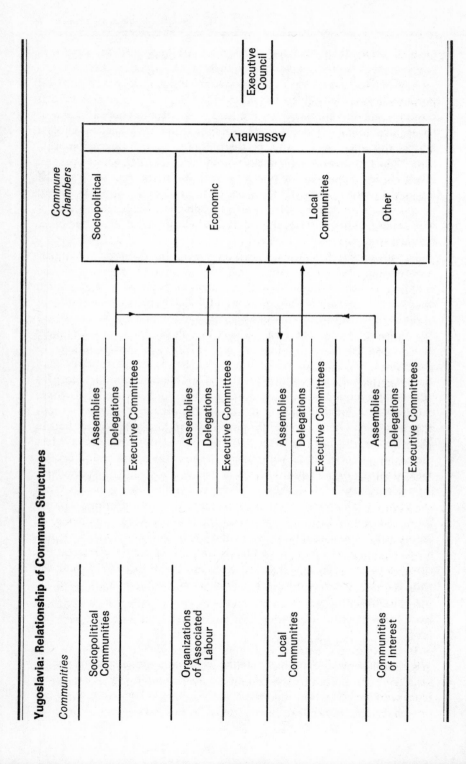

Communities

Commune Chambers

Sociopolitical Communities

Organizations of Associated Labour

Local Communities

Communities of Interest

Assemblies
Delegations
Executive Committees

Assemblies
Delegations
Executive Committees

Assemblies
Delegations
Executive Committees

Assemblies
Delegations
Executive Committees

Sociopolitical

Economic

Local Communities

Other

ASSEMBLY

Executive Council

agencies. That is, there are representatives of clients and professionals, with equal rights though perhaps not equal numbers. Representatives of consumers, however, may not be direct consumers, but the community at large represented through their delegates in work organizations: a system reminiscent of Sweden's use of unions to represent consumer interest. The communities of interest exist at both the level of the Commune and of the Republic, and possibly also the Federation. The Community for Child Care (a sub-group of the Community for Social Welfare) exists at the geographic and political level of the Commune for purposes of direct care and services to children, but at the level of the Republic for financial programs (which include Family Allowance). The republic-level Community Assembly also has its own staff chamber and a chamber of delegates from each commune-level community. It derives its status and authority from commune-level communities.

The consumer representatives in the commune-level Assembly of the Community are elected from two sources: the basic work organizations, and the local communities, each of which sends a delegate. Again, these delegates may vary personally according to the subject. In addition, the organizations' own workers are represented in a second "house" or chamber of the Community of Interest. When an issue is debated in the Commune (government) Assembly concerning it, the child-care community is considered a constituent part of the Assembly, and will have a representative to act as spokesman, with full voting rights, even though it will not be represented at another meeting.

Communities for health, likewise, are organized at the commune level with delegates from work organizations and local communities, and from staffs of health agencies. They are constituent members of the commune assembly, but participate only when health issues are discussed. The commune assembly may not decide on a health issue without the recommendation of the health community, except that in budget matters the commune assembly must make a final allocation of funds, and may reject the community's application for funds at the level requested. Regional and republic communities of health are made up of representatives of commune-level communities of health, and exist for purposes of coordination and representation at the republic level.

By comparison, there is only one community for pensions in Slovenia, and in most republics, with a republic-level assembly. Representatives are elected by the commune-level "conference of delegates" from work organizations and local communities. In Slovenia there are only sixty communes, but ninety chairs in the Assembly of the Community for Pensions, so the extra thirty chairs are distributed among the most heavily populated communes.

Trade Unions: Socio-Political Organizations

Syndicates, or unions, have a special place in the political and work system, not, as in western countries, to act in collective bargaining or otherwise defend workers against management (since they elect the managers and vote on policy) but to defend the principle of self-management. Their main duty seems to be educational, or political; to guard and stimulate the mechanisms of self-management by generating discussion. A by-product of this main function seems to be that the union helps workers to establish priorities among the very wide range of competing demands for support coming to them, not only with respect to the operation of the organization itself, but also from the community at large—issues of maintenance of the public services, via communities of interest, or of government, at any of the three levels. In effect, the unions seem to offer a vehicle for carrying political issues to almost the entire working population.

Union members have several channels for participation in policy-making: they elect delegates to the commune economic chamber, to the sociopolitical chamber, and to the communities of interest. In addition, they can share in elections in their locality of residence, for representatives to the commune chamber of local communities.

The Courts

Finally, there is a system of courts. These comprise not only the formal or "regular" courts set up by federal or republic authority for criminal and civil actions, but tribunals or "self-management courts" for arbitration or conciliation (between and) within work organizations and communities of interest. They are set up by the organizations themselves for the resolution of differences in claims or jurisdictions. These courts may consist of judges, or of working people themselves; in any case they have full authority within their jurisdictions. There is also the office of "social attorney for self-management" with duties like that of ombudsman, but especially directed to issues of protection of self-management rights.

Wage Rates and Social Budgeting

Salaries and wages are set by the workers in each work organization, subject to the limitations of their own resources and to maximum and minimum rates that are agreed by the mediation of unions, and other bodies. In each republic, unions are organized within a number of occupational or product specializations and these are united at commune and republic levels. They help to establish uniformity of pay scales for jobs at all levels. In some industries pay is calculated by setting a number of "points" for a job category. The actual wage varies with the organization's income and cost of living. The overall range in a large plant, from top to bottom, was of the order of 4.5:1.

A large number of groups representing different professions or trades meet with related groups to establish recommendations on wage rates. Each work organization's members contribute to discussion on these proposals; and they are all finally submitted to four authoritative groups at the republic level: the Republic Executive Council, the unions, the Socialist Alliance, and the Economic Chamber. Standard rates are set in this manner for general salary rates or professional tariffs, in each profession or industry, along with other budget standards, including service fees payable to health and welfare institutions and the social insurance rates charged against each industry. Budgets for public service communities are developed jointly in the first place by their staffs, with professional advice; then passed to the community assemblies to which they belong; then to joint meetings with other communities. Finally, they are referred back to work organizations and unions, before final submission for approval by the four republic level bodies mentioned above. This is a long process, designed to ensure thorough understanding and the greatest possible consensus on the ultimate policy. The system attempts to provide for maximum local participation in policy-making, but within the larger need for limitation of disparities of wealth and benefits between organizations, industries, and regions. What is created is a complex system of claims and counter-claims, with many people carrying out overlapping roles of workers, consumers, and political delegates.

This system has not yet come into full force, and its effect on social security programs is hard to assess. A major problem in the system to date has been the differences of productivity between industries, and therefore of the amounts available for wages and other benefits. A consequent problem has been the discomfort of government at all levels in trying to encourage equalization and redistribution by agreement, without transgressing their own policies of decentralization of decision-making. The new Constitution seeks to effect better distribution and equalization by diffusing power to many people and at the same time relating economic and political decisions at ground level: that is, getting people to make their own policies and deal with the consequences.

THE LABOUR FORCE

The population of Yugoslavia in 1971 was about 20,522,000, of whom 7,843,000 were described as agricultural. The economically active population numbered almost 9 million (8,890,000), of whom the agricultural workers were 3,900,000. About a million workers were employed abroad. The average total through 1972 of non-agricultural workers was 4,115,000, of whom 32.4 percent were women. About 3.5 million people were in "economically productive" or industrial work, and over 600,000 in the "noneconomic" clinical, business, and professional sector.[1] Over 1,614,000 people were over age 65, many of them receiving pensions; and over 8 million were dependents, including children.

INCOMES

Though it might be expected that income levels would be relatively even among workers in Yugoslavia, in fact there are notable differentials among regions, educational levels, types of industry, and occupations, which constitute a major policy problem. Each republic sets a legal maximum and minimum for the wage received from the primary place of employment. The monthly national minimum is 1,200 dinars.[2] The maximum may be about 8,000 dinars. This does not prevent additional earnings from secondary jobs, sales, and other such occupations, so that total income can in fact go over ten times the maximum. But this would be very rare. Average net personal receipts in 1971 were 1,432 din. per month and for 1972, 1,676 din. The average for "economically employed" or "socially productive" workers, such as those in industry or agriculture, was about 1,600 din. in 1972, and for those in "noneconomic" service trades and commerce was 1,900 din. The overall high average income by industry, in the economic sector, was in the petroleum industry at 2,230 din. and the low in textiles at 1,340 din. In the noneconomic sector, the high was in "economic chambers" (commercial institutions), at 2,560 din. and the low in cultural and educational institutions at 1,830 din.

Despite the generally low rewards for teachers, educational level or qualifications revealed further advantages for qualified people in certain fields. In 1971, differentials between so-called economic and noneconomic sectors did not significantly affect wage levels, but education did so, *within* sectors.

Table 5.1 **Effect of Education and Type of Industry on Wage Levels, 1971**

Highly Qualified	Highest		Lowest	
Economic sector	Industrial design	3,766 din.	Road transport	2,235 din.
Noneconomic sector	Social Insurance	3,463	Primary teacher	2,103
Unqualified				
Economic sector	Seaman	1,644	Textiles	931
Noneconomic sector	Lottery Operator	1,689	Primary teacher	825

Source: *Yugoslav Statistical Yearbook 1973*, Tables 122.2, 122.3.

Taking into account both the industry and educational level, the range of averages thus went from 3,766 din. a month to 825 din. The actual individual distributions were of course even greater.

The distribution curve for both sectors was rather steeply concentrated around 1,000–2,500 din. In 1972 the working population was distributed by income levels as seen in table 5.2.

However, chances of getting high pay were better in the "noneconomic sector". Much higher percentages of noneconomic than economic workers received higher salaries, with a modal range of 1,601–2,500 din. for the noneconomic as against 1,001–1,600 din. for economic workers.

Table 5.2 **Distribution of Working Population by Income Levels** (Percentage)

Income	Economic Sector	Noneconomic Sector
Under 600 din.	.4	.2
601–1000	13.5	8.3
1001–1600	45.3	32.4
1601–2500	30.7	41.3
2501–4000	8.8	14.7
Over 4000	1.3	3.1

Source: *Yugoslav Statistical Yearbook 1973*, Table 122.7.

The highest percentages in high-income levels of the noneconomic workers were found in commercial institutions, where almost 50 percent were paid over 2,500 din, and over 10 percent got over 4,000 din. The lowest category of all was the "other social service" workers (presumably unskilled institutional workers) of whom 41.6 percent got under 1,000 din. and only 2.8 percent got over 2,500 din. As a group, therefore, highly skilled workers in certain fields got four to five times the salaries of some low-skilled workers.

The distinction between economic and noneconomic sectors was dropped with the adoption of the new Constitution, presumably to avoid the political overtones of such terminology, in keeping with the unification of political and economic policy. Possibly, too, the preponderance of high salaries in the noneconomic sector might be an embarrassing conceptual paradox.

Regional incomes also showed differences.[3] Against a national average of 1,676 din., 1972 overall (rounded) averages for the republics and regions are shown in table 5.3.

Table 5.3 **Average Wages, by Republic**

Bosnia-Hercegovina	1,580 din.
Montenegro	1,470
Croatia	1,840
Macedonia	1,410
Slovenia	1,930
Kosovo	1,400
Serbia proper	1,570

These differences show up within occupations. For example, industrial designers in Slovenia got 3,510 din. a month, but in Macedonia got only 1,870 din. Textile workers in Slovenia got 1,644 din. but in Montenegro only 1,080 din. Teachers got 2,300 din. in Slovenia but only 1,430 din. in Kosovo. On the other hand, efforts at adjustment were taking place, relative to the Consumer Price Index. Taking the CPI for 1971 = 100, and the wage index = 100, the overall indices for Yugoslavia as a whole for both prices and wages were 117 for 1972. But the wage index for Slovenia was 118 and for Macedonia 119–120, so that some very slight real gains were made, in certain areas, reducing regional differences.

The incomes of families reflect the same income distributions as for individuals.[4] Many wives work, so that family incomes are relatively high. The average income of three-member families for the whole country in 1972 was 2,756 din., compared with the national individual average of 1,676 din. Against this, the average for the highest region, Slovenia, was 3,370 din. and for the lowest, Macedonia, only 2,070 din.[5] Although incomes are not reported by sex, it may be concluded that women's incomes made up the difference between individual and family income, and that the national average for women, therefore, would be about 1,100 din. compared with the men's average of 1,670 din. Four-member families did not do much better, with a national average of 2,767 din.—only 11 din. more than three-member families.[6] Presumably this is because there are normally only two workers in the family regardless of the number of children; although, given the shortage of housing, it might be expected that there would often be several earners in a single household.

These amounts do not seem large, but they are sufficient, given cost-levels, to permit substantial savings, averaging from 10 percent to 20 percent of earnings. Average family earnings for Yugoslavia being 2,756 din., savings in 1972 were 381 din. a month. In Slovenia, savings were 590 din. a month and in Montenegro 222 din.

As to costs, food and drink were the largest single budget items, amounting to an average 957 din. (about 30.3 percent of the budget) for the country. Unlike household budgets in Canada, rent, fuel, light, and furnishings amounted only to 12.6 percent of budget, at 285 din. Clothing and transportation each took about 220 din., and loan repayments were surprisingly high, on average, at 292 din. Regional differences in expenditure closely followed the regional differences in incomes outlined above. For example, housing costs in Slovenia were about 420 din. but in Macedonia only 290 din. Food costs in Slovenia were 1,030 din., but in Macedonia 795 din. (all for a family of three).[7] Naturally, the proportions of income spent on essential items varied with income level. Three-member families with less than 1,400 din. a month spent over 40 percent of their budget on food and drink, and over 12 percent on housing, while those at the highest income levels (over 5,000 din. a month) spent only 24 per cent on food and drink. But the housing system resulted in fairly equitable costs, so that high-income people still paid about 12 percent. However, the lowest levels still somehow managed to save almost 10 percent against the highest group's 15 percent.

Clearly, income differentials (and therefore social security benefits) across the country are quite marked. They are related to the technological development of the region, to the type of industry, and to level of education. Family incomes are much higher than individual incomes. In most families there is more than one earner, and income support programs are designed on the traditional assumption of responsibility of the extended family. Budget items follow income differences, with especial difficulty for the poorest-paid in regard to their food costs, but still apparently affording a living income for the great majority. Low housing costs seem to have a great deal to do with this rather satisfactory picture.

CHAPTER SIX

Social Security Programs in Yugoslavia

UNEMPLOYMENT INSURANCE

Former Republic laws established Republic Institutes for Employment, but the powers and duties were turned over to communes that assigned a proportion of their income to the Republic Institute. Under the new Constitution, these Institutes have now become Communities for Employment, one of five sub groups of the Community for Social Welfare. Contributions for the program are assessed against work organizations (thus covering all workers in "social" enterprises), at the rate of to between .5 percent and 1.5 percent of payroll.

Eligibility and Use

The costs of unemployment insurance are quite limited because of very stringent eligibility conditions. Formerly, the worker must have worked at least one year continuously or eighteen months in the previous two years. Now there is no time requirement, but there are other limits to eligibility. The worker must register with the communal employment centre within thirty days, and his resources, combined with those of any family members to whom he might look for help, must not exceed a level set by the Community. He may not have been dismissed for cause, or have quit except for cause.

The result of these restrictions is that although at the end of December 1972 there were officially 333,500 unemployed, only 10,200 were receiving unemployment insurance.[1] The unemployment rate is conservatively estimated at at least 7 percent. Over half of the un-employed were under 24 years of age and many were seeking work for the first time. Lacking work experience, they were not eligible for in-surance payments. The problem of new entrants to the labour force seems acute, in part perhaps because of the relative security of job tenure, once people are accepted. That is, the labour market is not expanding as fast as the labour force, and turnover is discouraged by the principle of "membership" in industry. Other unemployed people had other family income, especially from husbands or wives, so were ineligible. Unemployment insurance is used, in effect, like a rather strict means-tested assistance program. Over half of the recipients had been receiving insurance payments for less than five months, so that few cases approximated maximum use.

Benefits

Benefits in general amounted to about 50 percent of the individual's average wage for the preceding three months, but the amount could be increased by the commune. In Slovenia[2] the minimum is 700 din. and the maximum 2,000 din. per month. Duration of benefit varies with work history. In 1974 it was a minimum of 6 months if the recipient had worked the minimum of one year before, 12 months if he had worked for 30 continuous months before, or for 50 months in the preceding 5 years; 18 months' benefit for 5 to 10 years' work, and 24 months for over 10 years' work. Benefits continue during retrain-ing arranged by the Employment Centre. Benefits may also include 50 percent of the cost-of-moving expenses for the family, and a lump sum decided by the commune. Health benefits are automatically pre-served while the man receives unemployment insurance.

Placement and Training

The commune employment office is responsible for job placement and for retraining programs, as well as for unemployment insurance. There is a professional advisory council concerned especially with placement and training. Training takes place largely within work organizations, and the cost is shared by the individual work organization and the employment community. A man cannot be forced to take a job below the one he had or for which he is trained, but the employment com-munity is also the primary body responsible for judging "job equiv-alence" relative to eligibility for insurance. The community would be able to insist on a man taking the job offered, but there is an appeal procedure, to the Workers' Assembly. Although appeals are rare, they are apparently an effective defence of worker rights because of the sympathy of co-workers in the Community Assembly. Officials are therefore careful, tending towards generous interpretation of the rules. The employment office staff, rather than the unemployed worker, may be blamed for failure or injustice.

All hiring is not done through employment institutes or communities, since enterprises take on workers directly. This process is not so much "hiring", as admission to membership, because of the philosophy of worker management. Once the worker is accepted, it is only for serious cause that he will be terminated. Enterprises must do all they can to find alternative jobs or retraining within the plant if a worker is unsatisfactory in a given job. This in part explains why young people make up such a large proportion of the unemployed.

The employment community tries to plan proper manpower use in its area. In Ljubljana (Slovenia), the centre tests the entire population of school-leaving students. It discusses the job market with school officials and may influence school programs, in the choice of trades training offered.

HEALTH INSURANCE

Coverage

Each republic in Yugoslavia has responsibility to authorize the establishment of self-governing Health Insurance Communities, which include, broadly, the health insurance organizations, health care organizations, and health workers. Under the new Constitution, basic communities of health are established at the commune level. They come together at regional and republic levels for planning, coordinating, and supervising health care. Health care is negotiated by agreements between health institutions and insurance associations. Generally, health communities are set up for workers in three separate work categories (though in Slovenia these are combined in one): (1) workers in basic work organizations (mainly industrial and commercial), (2) farmers, (3) groups of professional individuals or businessmen.

These groups, whether as employers or self-employed individuals, are compelled to contribute to health insurance for all persons employed. Any who are not compulsorily covered in these categories are entitled to health care either by voluntary coverage, or, if they lack funds, by commune finances. Commune coverage extends to full-time

Table 6.1 **Persons Covered by Health Insurance, 1971**

Active contributors	4,872,433
Old age, disability, or family pensions	1,176,128
Temporarily unemployed	71,274
Contributors Total	6,119,835
Dependents	8,025,551

Source: *Yugoslav Statistical Yearbook 1973*, Table 123.3.

volunteers, students or trainees, temporarily unemployed persons who were previously insured, and unemployed youth. The dependents of contributors or beneficiaries are also covered, including divorced spouses responsible for children. In effect, the total population is at least theoretically eligible for basic care.

Each health community must cover a territory that includes at least 150,000 workers (potential if not actual members). The intention under the new Constitution is that each commune should have a community of health. Communes cover both urban and rural areas, so that the entire country is served. The total number of people covered by health insurance is over 14 million. The rest (mainly peasants not organized in cooperative forms) are covered for health care by other provisions.

Contributions

The system of contributions to health insurance emphasizes the principle of community, unifying the individual's central activity of work, or study, or retirement with the satisfaction of needs. Contributions come from employing organizations and institutions for all their workers. The source for others is not "the government" but their primary organizational association. It is striking that schools and universities contribute for their students and apprentices, local employment associations for unemployed people, and pension and invalid associations for their beneficiaries. Farmers may pay a percentage of their farming income.

Contributions must cover not only all operating costs, but also enough for a reserve fund for contingencies. In addition, and most important in a society that puts such weight in the idea of decentralization and autonomy, each association must have a "solidarity fund" used to equalize finances among associations. This is one of the mechanisms by which unity and collective responsibility are assured.

Farmers' solidarity funds are subsidized by the Republic and commune communities for health, for reallocation to equalize the resources of farmers' associations. This is done by agreement or by self-taxation of industrial workers, not by a tax imposed by central government. Regional communities of health contribute to and administer their own solidarity funds. With the exception of the farmers' solidarity funds then, for benefits and administration, costs are met from contributions, a large portion of which are treated as part of the operating costs of industry and service organizations.

In Slovenia, farmers and workers were united when the new Constitution was adopted, in 1974, in all regional communities for health; so farmers now have equal rights to health services. Their contributions, however, are set at half the rate for workers, because they do not receive cash sickness benefits.

Health care is extended to noncontributors at the expense of communes, if it is shown that they have no means of support or responsible family members. The specific terms of eligibility and services are approved by the commune assembly after proposal by the community of health. An exception is that care of dangerous mental patients is charged to the Republic. Persons otherwise uninsured but with the means to do so may take out voluntary insurance.

In addition to the regular payroll contribution, there is a small user charge for health services.[3]

Table 6.2 **User Charges for Health Services, Slovenia 1974**

Prescription	5 din.
Home visit	10
Office or clinic call	5
Specialist fee (if referred)	5
Specialist fee (not referred)	30
Ambulance	10
Hearing aids, etc.	10
Abortion	150
Alcoholic treatment	50

Dental care user charges were higher: 30 percent of the fee for major work, 20 percent for minor treatment, 10 percent for prophylactic care and examination. Medical and dental services are free to children and pensioners, however.

Contribution Rates and Costs

Depending on the costs and the benefits decided by the association beyond statutory minima, contribution rates for health and sickness insurance (including work injuries), vary from about 7 percent to 9 percent of gross payroll. About 1 percent goes to solidarity funds to equalize services. Pensions and invalidity take approximately 12 percent of gross, and child care costs (including family allowance contributions) about 9 percent. The national average for all social insurance runs at about 31 percent. This does not include allocations for housing and for various fringe benefits. Thus total costs are divided into three roughly equal parts: pensions and disability, health care, and child care. Slovenian associations for these major programs decided in 1974 to set a maximum of 35 percent of gross payroll for all costs.

Taking $1971 = 100$, the 1972 consumer price index was 117. But the amounts devoted to various cash benefit programs rose much more steeply, suggesting a change in policy.

Table 6.3 **Cost Indices of Major Benefit Programs, 1972**
$(1971 = 100)$

Consumer price index	117
Cash sick pay, work injury	135
Maternity leave pay	135
Invalidity, old age pensions	128
Survivor pensions	132

The total cost in 1972 of health insurance, for Yugoslavia as a whole, including administration, re-insurance, etc., was 2,364 din. per contributor (index 125) and the cost of pensions, including administration, was 3,671 din. per contributor (index 130).[4]

Benefits

Basic health care specified by republic law is very broad, including maternity care, dental care for young people, even to age 26 for students. At user charges listed in table 6.4, health services include prevention and treatment of a wide range of diseases, and work-related illness or injury, including cost of travel for treatment. Injured workers retain their insured status.

Sick benefit is paid to injured or sick workers, and, as in Sweden,

Table 6.4 **Yearly Costs of Medical Care per Contributor, Yugoslavia** (in Dinars)

	Amount	Index (1971=100)
Clinic and dispensary	509 din.	129.5
Dental care	97	115.5
Fixed clinics and hospitals	753	118.2
Prescriptions	331	129.8
Sick and injury pay	273	135.1
Pregnancy	120	134.8
Birth grant	6	120.0
Funeral	10	120.0
Total, including administration	2,364 din.	124.7

to any person who must look after a sick child or any sick member of his or her immediate family. Local communities of health decide on the amount of sickness benefit to be paid, but it is in no case less than 60 percent of the individual's average wage for the preceding year, and is often more. The employer must normally pay sick benefit as wages for the first 30 days, insurance picking up the cost thereafter.

Compensation is very generous for certain special categories. It is 100 percent of average wages for the preceding year for occupational injury or disease, for trainees and apprentices, and for mothers during 105 days of pregnancy, delivery, and post-natal period. After 105 days, a mother may receive 50 percent of wages up to the eighth month. A full wage allowance is also made to the mother for care of a sick child under age 3. A cash grant is made for each birth, and for funeral costs.

The amount of sick cash benefit increases with the length of illness. For example, in Ljubljana, the rates (as of 1973) are shown in table 6.5.

Table 6.5 **Sickness Benefit Rates**

Length of Sickness	Benefit Payable	
	Insured over 6 months	Insured less than 6 months
First 7 days	70%	60%
8–60 days	80	70
Over 60 days	90	90

If the recipient is in hospital, the rate drops by 10 percent. In Serbia and Croatia, the rate may in no case be less than 70 percent of wages. In cash terms, the average daily sick benefit amounted to 46 dinars.

If there is dispute about the benefit, or eligibility, appeals are possible at two levels: one, to a special authority of the health association's general assembly, and second, to the communal court.

PENSIONS AND INVALIDITY INSURANCE

Administration

A federal Law of 1972 requires republics to assure provision of pensions, and all republics do so by republican laws, assigning administrative responsibility to pension and disability insurance communities, which are similar to the communities for health insurance but not so numerous. Basically there is one main community in each republic, but large cities are treated as autonomous, and have their own communities. There are branches of the republic-level community in different regions, acting as local administrative and consultative bodies. Local autonomy is thus not the same in pension insurance as in health communities, since even detailed provisions are set by the republic-level community. In Serbia, for example, there are only eight branch pension associations. Federal law specifies that the republic communities must offer the following basic provisions: old age pension; disability pension, including vocational rehabilitation and cash compensation for loss of work capacity; cash compensation for injury; family (survivors') pension.

Coverage

Insured persons include all workers in enterprises or institutions who are employed at least half-time, public servants, craft workers and fishermen, disabled persons, apprentices or others undergoing training.

In 1972 the number of active insurance contributors in Yugoslavia was 4,969,200. The major beneficiary classes were for old age, disability, and survivors. The beneficiaries listed in Table 6.6 are, of course, not all permanent pensioners.

Table 6.6 **Pension Recipients, 1972**

Program	Beneficiaries
Invalid pensions	430,985
Cash payments, invalids	105,403
Payments in kind, invalids	3,552
Temporary compensation	10,638
Reduced work compensation	14,079
Reduced income compensation	14,154
Old age pensions	476,946
Family (survivors') pensions	319,319
Total pensions	1,227,250

Source: Yugoslav Federation of Pension and Health Insurance, *Review of Basic Social Insurance for 1972*, Tables B.39, B.40.

Eligibility

Old age pensions may be drawn at age 60 for men (55 for women) after at least 20 years of contributions, or at age 65 (60) after 15 years, but not if the person continues to work. They may be drawn at any age after 40 years' contributions (35 years for women).

Disability pension may be either work-related or not. If the injury was not work-related, full disability pension is available only if the claimant has contributed three-quarters of the time since the age of 20 and if disablement is complete, or if the injury was sustained at an age when there is not the possibility of vocational rehabilitation. If the injury was work-related, there is no required time of contribution. If disablement is partial and/or rehabilitation is possible, other benefit programs are applied, such as temporary or reduced work compensation. Eligibility may be established even if contributions are for less than three-quarters of the time since age 20, if they are concentrated in a way satisfactory to the commune, and especially if the disabled person is under age 30.

Family pensions are payable to survivors (immediate family) if the deceased was insured for at least five years and if his contributions were concentrated in an order approved by the commune, or was qualified for pension after 20 years' work, or was otherwise receiving or entitled to old age pension or injury compensation. If the death resulted from work-related injury or illness, no qualifying period is required.

A widow may receive pension if she is at least 45 years old, or at a younger age if she is incapable of working, or has dependent children requiring her care. She can retain a permanent pension if the children become independent only after she is 40. Similarly, provision is made for male survivors. A widower who was dependent on his wife can receive pension if he is age 60, or incapable of work, or has dependent children. A child is eligible for pension to age 15, and the deceased's parents are eligible if they are 60 (for the father) or 45 (for the mother), or incapable of work.

Eligibility for pension depends on contributions made on the worker's behalf during a "qualifying period." This period may be fulfilled under various circumstances:

a) full-time work, means not only that exact condition but includes

1. those working to the limits of their capacity, if disabled,
2. half-time disabled servicemen,
3. insured women nursing or caring for a child;

b) part-time work if it totals at least half-time, even if spent with more than one employer;

c) periods of compensated sickness;

d) time spent on vocational rehabilitation after being disabled for work;

e) time spent on retraining or specialization;

f) time spent on unpaid leave from work under supervision, or in prison;

g) time spent serving in the armed forces;

h) periods covered by voluntary contributions;

i) for 30 days after loss of work if worker is registered at an employment office.

Certain employment, in dangerous or unhealthy conditions, is credited at a preferred rate for purposes of calculating qualification. The place of work as a criterion of eligibility in all these programs is very clear.

Contributions

Rates of contributions to the pension funds are decided by the republic-level community for pensions, in consultation with local communes, work organizations, trade unions, and republic authorities. Generally, in 1972, the rate was about 12 percent of gross payroll, but is rising. The rate anticipated for Slovenia in 1975 was 14.4 percent. Funds are centralized within each republic-level community for pensions, for purposes of determining policy on costs and benefits. There is no capital accumulation except for a small reserve fund.

Contributions are made by all work organizations, (employers), by self-employed persons, by individuals for voluntary coverage, and by public authorities responsible for different categories of people who are eligible for coverage but not working. The average cost of benefits in 1972 for the country (per insured contributor) varied with the program, and in most programs outran the consumer price index.

Benefits

Pension benefits are calculated on a base of the individual's previous ten years' average income, revalued to the last 2 years' living cost levels. The maximum amount of old age pension and invalidity pension (for full entitlement) is 85 percent of the base, reduced proportionately according to reduced years of contributions or lesser degrees of disability. Family (survivors) pension may be up to 100 percent of the pension entitlement. The minimum (available after 20 years' work) is 55 percent of the base wage for men and 45 percent for women. Two percent is added for each year's work, to the 85 percent maximum after 35 years. Pensions are paid only on application, after retirement, and retirement is not compulsory except after 40 years.

The cash amount of benefits varies among programs and republics. Each of the major programs has a supplementary payment, which

Table 6.7 Pensions and Invalidity Insurance Yearly Costs per Contributor, 1972 (in Dinars)

	Amount	Index (1971=100)
Invalidity pension	863	127.9
Cash invalidity pay	17	113.3
Blind and disabled supplement	20	133.3
Special supplement, invalids	30	120.0
Old age pension	1,464	128.1
Old age supplement	8	114.3
Family pensions	547	131.8
Family pension supplement	3,671	129.2

Source: Federation of Pensions and Health Insurance, *Review of Basic Social Insurance for 1972*, Tables A.31–A.34.

should be included to estimate the actual value. The average old age pension for Yugoslavia in 1972, including supplements, was about 1,410 din., compared with a family pension and supplement of about 830 din. and a disability pension of 940 din. Furthermore, the amounts vary between republics. The average old age pension in Serbia was about 1,440 din., but in Montenegro only about 1,025 din. On the other hand, family pensions in Serbia averaged 800 din. and in Montenegro 900 din.[5] All of these amounts are considerably less than the average wages for each republic. The closest approximation to average wages was in Serbia, where the average wage was 1,573 din. and old age pension 1,440 din., but in Slovenia where the average wage was 1,936 din., the old age pension was 1,390 din. and the disability pension only 980 din. In effect, benefit differences between republics are less than wage differences, probably due to benefit equalization policies.

In addition to cash benefits, the community for pensions provides funds for housing for pensioners. Four percent of the total value of pension paid is allocated to housing funds. These funds are allocated to each of the commune-level communities on the basis of the percentage of pensioners in each. Most of the money is used to build or operate homes for aged or disabled people who have not already their own or family homes.

OTHER BENEFITS

Family Allowances

Family allowances are not universal, but are used as family income supplements subject to a means test. The program is administered by local pensions and invalidity associations and is financed by charges against enterprises. Contributions and general policy are decided by the republic-level communities for social welfare, and vary from 1.2 percent of payroll in the wealthier republics to 3.7 percent in Macedonia. The republic community sets the maximum benefits but the local groups may vary the amount. In Ljubljana, one of the more affluent centres, the means test is set at 900 din. per family member per month. When the income is between 600 din. and 900 din., the benefit is a basic amount of 95 din. for the first child and 150 din. for each subsequent child. Higher supplements of 160 din. for the first and 240 din. for each subsequent child are provided when other income falls below 600 din. Unwed mothers may receive 30 percent more than the basic rate, and parents of handicapped children may receive an additional 50 percent. The number of families receiving family allowance is rather small in affluent areas: about 12 percent of workers and 4.7 percent of pensioners in Ljubljana. In 1971, however, beneficiary families numbered 762,000, with 1,702,000 children for the country as a whole, at a cost of about 700 din. per child for the year.[6]

Housing

Under the new Constitution, communities for housing are set up as one of the sub-groups of the community for social welfare. Their major objective is to provide housing for low - income and aged persons, and for young couples. In the last group, priority is given to young couples with children, who have worked at least five years. There is no income test for families. There is a limit, however, for low-income and aged people, of 900 din. per person in the household. These people are handled by collaboration between the communities of Housing and Social Care.

In addition to building housing units, the community turns back part of its fund to assist work organizations with their own housing plans, and to help in the repair and maintenance of existing housing.

The funds for housing come, like all other social programs, from industry. By agreement, every enterprise sets aside a fixed percentage of its total payroll for housing. The amount of the fund, decided collectively by the enterprise, the communal assembly, and the unions, runs at about 4.5 percent to 7.5 percent of payroll. Just over half of this goes to the community for housing, and the remainder is at the disposal of the firm.

A well-established firm in Ljubljana[7] provided housing to its workers either by assigning company-owned flats, to those who lacked the equity for a payment on their own, or by providing 25-year loans at low interest (about 2 percent). The majority of users received the loan credits. If a worker works for the company for at least 10 years, he may be granted ownership of the assigned flat. Of the total fund set up by the firm for all fringe benefits, about one-third goes to housing. In addition, a portion of the assessment for pensions and invalidity insurance is allocated to housing for these pensioners.

Housing is in short suppy despite a policy of encouragement to private building contractors. In 1970, over half of the investment capital in housing was private; but, with the establishment of the new communities, it is likely that public housing will again take precedence. Workers get housing (mostly in the form of flats) through employers, but may apply directly to the community for housing. Because of a combination of factors—lack of capital and poor building technology —housing is in short supply and units tend to be reserved for long-term workers.[8] Nonetheless, housing costs are not a high proportion of family budgets, averaging (as seen above) 12.6 percent.[9]

Social Help

Responsibility for social assistance is assigned by the Constitution to the communes. The community of social welfare includes a sub-community of social care responsible for all social work services and social assistance. Policy is referred, as with other communities, to the commune assembly for approval. As elsewhere, social aid is a program generally run, except for some special categories, on "less eligibility" principles. That is, it is awarded only when all else fails and at rates well below wages.

Republic laws repeat that the purpose of aid is to restore people to work. Aid is usually given only if there is no one in the family able to work (75 percent incapacity), for children under 15, or where necessary, to mothers during a 135 day period around childbirth. However, in more affluent areas, an income test rather than a work test is applied. Cash benefit amounts to 50 percent of minimum legal wage for the area, with supplements for blind, paralyzed, or severly ill persons. In addition, a lump sum may be given for clothing, and provision is made for housing free or at low rent, for those in need, vacations, and other services. Eligibility is dependent on income alone in Ljubljana, where the family is permitted up to 900 din. per member per month.

Fringe Benefits

In addition to their responsibility for financing statutory social security and housing programs, enterprises also establish discretionary or "consumption" funds for benefits for their own workers. The amount and use of such money varies with the enterprise. In addition to rent, renovation, and furnishing subsidies, the purposes include subsidized meals at plant restaurants, vacations (lump sum amounts of about 1,400–2,000 din. per year, or free care at company centres), union dues, scholarships and training programs, day care centres, recreation facilities public schools, special gifts or condolence money. Next to housing, vacations take the largest amount. Some firms maintain their own holiday resorts. Not surprisingly, the amount allocated by enterprises to consumption funds increases directly with the level of wages (and productivity) of the industry.[10] Poorer firms must allocate more of their product to wages to be competitive, and so skimp on fringe benefits.

CONCLUSIONS

Yugoslavs are well aware of the important variations of incomes and benefits among republics and even between regions within republics. The northern republics (Slovenia and Croatia) are more industrialized, and generally wages and benefits there far exceed those of the southern republics of Macedonia and Montenegro, or the autonomous province of Kosovo, in Serbia. Part of the problem is the concentration of peasant populations in the southerly and more mountainous regions. Within republics the difference between farmers and industrial workers is marked. To overcome these differences, there have for years been "solidarity funds" used for equalization. The principle of equalization funds is now found not only between and within republics, but even within enterprises, reflecting the principle of autonomy of self-managing sections of society or of industry, but also recognizing the need for mutual aid.

The problem of aged people is somewhat modified in Yugoslavia compared with other countries, because of the enormous respect accorded veterans of the Liberation War. However, other populations (such as the handicapped, women, young entrants to the labour force) still suffer from unequal benefits and opportunity. Various studies of social mobility and of participation show that movement is slow despite efforts to encourage involvement.[11] In this regard, Yugoslavia's problems are shared with most western countries as well as Japan.

The level of social security benefits is not so far behind average wages, nor so different from one area to another, as to create a sense of serious injustice between groups in the population. Furthermore, the differences of benefits among programs, or types of contingency, are not so great, with the exception of social aid. The effect of the new Constitution in uniting political, social, and economic decision-making has yet to be seen. But it seems that the way has been prepared for common principles of mutual concern to apply in these areas so as to reduce differentials as resources increase; or at least to share risks more equally. Admittedly, workers are well rewarded, as compared with nonworkers, and the economy is not so strong as to assure work to all who need it. Lack of work is the major problem in the way of full social democracy. How much of it is due to lack of centralist control of the economy, or conversely to lack of capitalist investment and incentives, is not possible to say. Yugoslavia's rate of growth and modernization has been rapid, but the existence of a large number of people untrained in industry and commerce no doubt has been a serious limitation. In any case the question to be answered is not so much whether the absolute level of resources and benefits is as high as in other modern countries, but whether access is equalized. In this respect the distribution of resources compares well with most western nations, and the distribution of powers is probably better.

Part 4

Japan

CHAPTER SEVEN

Japan: Work, Wages, and Government

The culture of Japan is probably as complex as any on earth, and is difficult for other nations to understand. This in itself is a source of bitterness to sensitive Japanese. Their values are the values of others, but carried to extremes become paradoxical and so create misunderstanding. The highest virtues lead to terror and death; the nation's heroes become suicides.

Like people of other nations, the Japanese value hard work, intelligence, beauty, self-discipline, and devotion. Perhaps above all they value loyalty. Historically, loyalty to the feudal lord came above all else. With the restoration of the Emperor to supreme authority a century ago, and the institutionalization of his divinity, loyalty to the Emperor was the first obligation of all Japanese; but this only confirmed the virtue of loyalty and deference to superiors at any rank. Though defeat in World War II stripped the Emperor of divinity, it did not do away with the ancient acceptance of hierarchical authority and the virtues of self-denial in a common cause. Loss of overseas land and resources compelled the Japanese to enter on an intense and enormously successful program of industrialization which has brought an affluence undreamed of at the height of military imperialism.

Loyalty to the firm, with mutual duties and rewards, is the central dynamic of modern Japan. This is not a democratic loyalty. It permits and assumes differences of rank and authority, and the centralization of power.

Nationally, power is centralized in an alliance of government and big business. This is possible despite the fact that the population is about five times that of Yugoslavia or Canada and over thirteen times that of Sweden, primarily because the people are racially and culturally very homogeneous. There are no significant minorities. It may also be because so much of the population is concentrated in the two megalopolitan areas of Tokyo and Osaka, which are themselves only three or four hours apart by rail. Services may be decentralized, but information and decisions can be centralized. Centralization is also a tradition since feudal times, when the Shōgun kept close control against revolts by his nobles.

The tradition of hierarchical accountability and devotion to one's superiors also helps to explain the existence of a large and effective bureaucracy at all levels of government, and even in business.

MAJOR STRUCTURES AND PROCESSES OF GOVERNMENT

The governmental structure of Japan is a constitutional monarchy similar to the British parliamentary system. There is a Diet of two elected houses; the house of representatives and the house of councillors. The house of representatives corresponds, with like powers, to the house of commons. The government, led by a prime minister, is formed by the majority party in the Diet.

Public administration is highly centralized, for although there are Prefectures, their powers are more like those of the Swedish counties as agents of central government, than of the Canadian provinces, but lack the "feed-back" mechanisms of Swedish county administration. Most of the social programs of government, including education, social security, and welfare, are carried or supervised directly by ministries of the national government, with their bureaucracies, so that regional and local offices and even the office of the prefectural governor are only extensions of the central power. Prefectural and metropolitan governments are required to establish and administer public and preventive health centres, maternal and child health programs, institutions of various kinds, child guidance centres, and public welfare offices. The prefectures and cities establish departments of health and welfare, under which are set up regional service centres at the rate of one for about 100,000 population. Costs of welfare are shared by the national and prefectural governments. About 80 percent of benefit costs come from national sources, but about two-thirds of health centres' operating costs are carried by prefectural or local governments.

A major responsibility of municipal governments is administration of national health insurance, under central government authority. One area where Japanese administration parallels that of Sweden is in the statutory requirement of representation of workers and employers in local and regional councils administering various labour laws such as those dealing with supervision of minimum wages and work conditions. However, the fragmented nature of Japanese trade unions in comparison with Swedish unions, greatly weakens the effect of worker participation, especially as the representatives are all government appointed.

The governments of Japan have always been relatively conservative, closely allied with large corporations. Socialist or communist groups, though very vocal, have little reliable support. Trade unions are divided. Less than 10 percent of the workers are organized in the major national federations of unions, and these are split between radical and conservative wings. There is no effective challenge either to government or employers. A possible reason for this is that unions are organized neither by trades nor by industries, but on a company basis, and though union demands are often influential at the company level, personal loyalty to the firm severely limits any union action. It is interesting that the membership of the largest and more radical federation, Sōhyō, is heavily made up of public employees, while the second largest, and more conservative federation, Dōmei, is made up mainly of employees in private firms. Sōhyō consistently takes radical leadership in demands for increased wages and other social reforms, but has been unable to make any serious impact on the balance of political power.

There are no such formal processes as are found in Sweden or Yugoslavia to encourage political participation by workers or protect the "little man." Despite this, the spirit of duty and efficiency, combined with traditions of paternalistic concern, have produced an effective network of social programs that compares well with countries that pride themselves on their democracy.

THE LABOUR FORCE AND WAGES

Japan's resurgence as a major world power, after World War II, is due largely to the successful development of high-level technology and maximum use of her expanding labour force. Two population problems have concerned the Japanese: first, to limit population growth, and second, to meet an anticipated shift in the population towards the upper age groups. The rate of growth was stabilized as of 1973, through limitation of family size (often by abortion) and the aging process does not yet affect the work force. In 1972 only about 7 percent were aged 65 or more.

Despite stabilization of the rate of growth, the population is enormous. It yields a large work force, but is a source of constant concern for the supply of raw materials and food. The population in 1972 was 107,330,000. Of these 80,510,000 were 15 years of age or more, and the work force was 51,820,000: almost half of the total population. The unemployed numbered only 730,000. By 1973 the work force had increased by a million, to 52,990,000, and unemployment had dropped to only 670,000, or about 1.3 per cent.[1] Competition for labour was severe, and especially for current high school and university graduates. One effect of this situation was that the tradition of lifetime attachment of employees to the firm is beginning to break down, with increasing numbers of transfers to better jobs within about five years of initial employment. This in turn has resulted in increasing disadvantage for smaller firms, unable to compete with the giants in wage levels and fringe benefits.

Japan's level of wages has risen with increasing speed over recent years, bringing living standards up to those of some European nations. But Japan has not escaped inflation; indeed it has been hit harder than most developed nations, with a rate of about 25 percent in 1974. By the end of 1974, too, higher unemployment rates were threatening as Japan suffered from the world-wide recession. But in general, wage rates kept ahead of price increases, with especially large real wage increases in 1973 and 1974.

In money terms, average cash earnings of full-time workers were about 85,000 yen per month in 1971 and 98,500 yen in 1972 (including bonuses). Casual and day workers' pay went from just over 1,500 yen per day in 1971 to 1,700 yen a day in 1972.

Table 7.1 **Earnings and Price Indices, 1970–1973**

	Cash Earnings	Consumer Price Index
1970	100	100
1971	114.7	106.1
1972	132.9	110.9
1973	161.7	125

$1. U.S.=about 300 yen. Income figures taken from *Yearbook of Labour Statistics*, 1972, Tables 42, 43, 115, 117, 118, 126.

On average, with several members working, family income was much higher than individual earnings, and allowed considerable savings. Total family income from all sources averaged 213,000 yen per month in 1972, while the main items of family living costs averaged 99,300 yen. Taxes were very low: only 6,750 yen (about 4.8 percent). Other costs, debts, premiums, insurance, and property purchase amounted to 24,200 yen. This left a surplus of over 80,000 yen. Of this about 48,000 yen was used as a monthly cushion, and real savings were of the order of 35,000 yen a month.

Wage Variables

Of course, these averages conceal great differences in wages and salaries and other types of income, that differ by a number of variables. Probably the most significant factor affecting income is sex, since men's salaries are always far higher than women's in all industries, of all sizes. The next most important variable is the size of firm. Large firms offer much greater benefits than do small firms, and this relationship is constant and predictable. Other factors affecting income are level of education, type of industry, worker's age (and seniority), and geographic region. The importance of the size of the firm is shown by the fact that while the mean total family income was over 213,600 yen a month in 1972, the figure varied from an average of about 152,200 yen for families whose heads worked in very small enterprises employing less than five workers, to 237,200 yen for those whose heads worked in large firms employing over 1,000 workers. Highest of all, at 239,000 yen, were the incomes of families whose heads were government workers.

It is noteworthy that workers in the smallest firms (5–29 employees) tend to get about the same wages in all industries, as contrasted with those in larger firms. In large companies, wages ranged from a low average of 112,000 yen a month in textiles, to a high of 190,000 yen in the financial businesses. Of course even more striking is the fact that women receive only about half the wages of men in all industries, and in all sizes of firms. Special wages, or bonuses, are even less for women, running at only one-third of that for men in the highest paying industry, finance, where presumably male status counts for more.

Bonuses and Budgets

A very important part of the Japanese wage system is the payment of two or three bonuses a year, and retirement allowances. The bonuses (or special wages) in large firms, again, constitute higher

Table 7.2 **The Effect of sex and size of Firm on average earnings in selected industries** (in '000's of yen)

	All Industries			Textiles		
No. of Workers	Total Wages	Con-tractual Wages	Special Wages	Total Wages	Con-tractual Wages	Special Wages
500 +						
male	130	94	36	112	84	28
female	70	50	20	49	39	10
100–499						
male	117	87	30	110	83	27
female	62	47	15	50	39	11
30–99						
male	110	83	27	99	80	19
female	60	45	15	43	35	8
5–29						
male	92	74	18	93	78	15
female	49	40	9	40	34	6
	Leather Products			Publishing		
500 +						
male	118	85	33	161	115	46
female	65	48	17	93	65	28
100–499						
male	98	75	23	120	88	32
female	49	39	10	71	50	21
30–99						
male	96	76	20	105	83	22
female	43	35	8	57	44	13
5–29						
male	103	87	16	96	79	17
female	48	42	6	50	42	8
	Finance and Insurance					
500 +						
male	192	119	73			
female	79	54	25			
100–499						
male	163	103	60			
female	73	52	21			
30–99						
male	152	101	51			

female	71	51	20
5–29			
male	120	82	38
female	60	44	16

Source: *Yearbook of Labour Statistics*, 1972, Table 43.

percentages of wages than do bonuses in small firms. That is, size of firm has even more effect on bonuses than on contractual wages. This is one of the ways companies create the ties of loyalty and obligation.

Bonuses are normally paid in March, June, and December. The largest is likely to be in December, when it may be double the monthly salary. For example one major company, perhaps a bit above average, pays a bonus of half a month's wage in March, 1.7 times the monthly wage in June, and 2.6 times in December, for a total of 4.8 times the monthly wage for the year. Employees thus receive almost 17 months' pay at the nominal wage for 12 months' work (in addition to paid vacation). In practice, bonuses are so well established as part of wage policy that they are the subject of union negotiation, and are generally calculated as part of cash wages.

Taxes, as indicated above, are relatively light. For families with income as low as 25,000 yen a month, monthly taxes are only 54 yen. The figure rises rather slowly at low incomes, until at 65,000 yen a month taxes are about 1,100 yen, at 150,000 are about 6,300 yen, and over 250,000 yen per month are still only 10 percent.[2]

As might be expected, the costs of food and housing bear most heavily on low-income people. In the case of housing, the burden is ameliorated by company support, but the disparity exists in part because better housing benefits are paid to the more highly paid workers in large companies than to those in small firms or to casual labour.

Table 7.3 **Contractual and Special Monthly Wages, by Size of Firm, 1972**

Size of Firm	Total Wages	Contractual	Special
500 +	114,429	82,741	31,688
100–499	99,632	74,035	25,597
30–99	92,405	69,753	22,652
5–29	75,010	60,478	14,532

Source: *Yearbook of Labour Statistics*, 1972, Table 43.

Food costs about half the income of those with low incomes of 25,000 yen, about a third at the level of 65,000 yen, about a fifth at 150,000 yen and less than a sixth at 250,000 yen. Housing costs much less: about one-seventh of family income at 25,000 yen, about a fifth at 65,000 yen, about a seventh at 150,000 yen and only about a ninth at 250,000 yen.[3]

NONWAGE LABOUR COSTS

Statutory benefits (social insurance, unemployment insurance, workmen's compensation), cost on average about 6 percent of all labour costs, nonstatutory benefits take from 3 to 4.5 percent, depending on the size of firm and type of industry. The average proportions of nonwage items for all industries are shown in table 7.4.

Table 7.4 **Distribution of Nonwage Costs, All Industries** (Percentage)

Retirement allowance	23.3%
Statutory benefits	37.2
Nonstatutory allowances	28.5
Benefits in kind (gifts etc.)	3.7
Vocational training	2.1
Recruitment	2.6
Other	2.6
	100%

Source: Ministry of Labour, Statistical Department, *Summary of Report on Employee Benefits and Labour Costs,* 1972.

As with bonuses, the total cost of fringe benefits increases with industry size. Firms employing over 1,000 people spend about 85 percent of all labour costs in wages and 15 percent in nonwage benefits, both statutory and voluntary. Small firms (30–100 employees) must spend more on wages to keep up, but then can afford less for fringe benefits. They spend 88 percent on wages and 12 percent on nonwage benefits. The benefits of smaller firms are very much less than those of large firms, because if they are to be at all competitive in wages, small firms cannot offer other bonuses. Even so the competition is very unequal; as we have seen, large firms pay much higher salaries

Table 7.5 **Indices of Cash Wages and Nonwage Costs by Size of Firm, 1972**

Size of Firm	Cash Wages	Nonwage Costs
1000 +	100	100
300–990	84	69
100–299	75	59
30–99	71	56

Source: Ministry of Labour, Statistical Department, *Summary of Report on Employees' Benefits and Labour Costs*, 1972.

as well as fringe benefits; hence the intense competition among workers to work for large firms, and the resulting concentration of power.

The wide ranges of wages and bonuses obviously create great differences in living standards by sex, size of industry, and type of industry. These differences are echoed in those social programs in which benefits are related to earnings, thus extending inequality rather than reducing it. The differences are especially marked in occupations that use seasonal or casual labour, such as agriculture and forestry, where workers are excluded from coverage by the main-line programs.

MANPOWER POLICY

Labour laws in Japan provide a wide-ranging series of programs of job training, placement service, relocation, employment stimulation, and emergency relief work that bear interesting comparison with those of Sweden. There is no doubt that they have been important in sustaining high productivity and raising standards of living. The network of employment exchanges (Public Employment Security Offices) is now computerized and nationally coordinated: it provides a very efficient aid to placement, and a series of training and relocation programs has been closely related to ensure efficient use of manpower. Because of the high employment rates, the system has not been under strain during the years ever since its formation in 1947.

Several important pieces of legislation govern manpower policies. The Labour Standards Law of 1947 deals with working conditions, hours of work, health, accident prevention, and compensation protection of women and children, minimum wages, living conditions, and workers' rights. It set up an inspection system under prefectural labour standards offices, and labour standards councils at both the national and prefectural levels under a national Director of Labour Standards. Prefectural offices may be supervised by regional offices. The members of labour standards councils are not autonomous, being appointed by the ministry, in equal numbers representing employers, workers, and "the public interest." Employers are required to keep accurate records of employment, wages, accidents, and all of the other areas covered in the Act.

A special Minimum Wages Law, of 1959, was passed to prescribe detailed procedures for minimum wage-setting, including both work in work places and at home. Minimum wages councils are set up within labour standards offices, at national and prefectural levels, with membership appointed as in the labour standards councils. Another Act on Labour Accident Prevention details the duties of the labour standards offices in this area.

A very important law is that on Employment Measures (of 1966). Its purpose is "to contribute toward the balanced development of the national economy and the achievement of full employment" through a series of provisions for placement, training, and job promotion. Specifically, it provides for vocational guidance and placement training and trades testing, interregional mobility, including provision of housing, and promotes employment of special groups like aging and physically handicapped workers.

Another major law is the Employment Security Law of 1947 that establishes the public employment security offices, and national and prefectural employment security councils, appointed in the same manner as the labour standards council. In addition to job placements and recruitment and unemployment insurance administration, the public employment security offices administer a special program for aiding interregional transfer of workers, and a program of unemployment relief projects for hard-to-place workers. Relief project workers are paid at prevailing rates. Special attention is given to older workers, who may receive living allowances and vocational training. Employers offering such services receive grants. This population is of particular concern because of the general practice in Japan of forced retirement at age 55. Since pensions are not payable until age 65, most of these workers must look for "post-retirement" jobs at lower pay. Special subsidies including capital grants are also paid to employers who hire handicapped workers.

The Employment Promotion Projects Corporation (1961) is a special program within the Ministry of Labour with responsibilty for vocational training, and the encouragement of labour mobility. Their options include low-cost housing construction to accommodate relocated workers. The law sets up three levels of vocational training centres. There are 285 general vocational training centres operated by prefectures. They offer basic courses and encourage private enterprise programs by sharing program materials and facilities. Ninety "advanced centres" are operated by the national Employment Promotion Projects Corporation, and 59 are operated by prefectures. Finally, an Institute of Vocational Training operated by the EPPC trains instructors for the other centres.

All of these laws help to protect workers' employability, and therefore they simultaneously ensure wages for the workers and skilled manpower for the nation.

CHAPTER EIGHT

Social Security Programs in Japan

UNEMPLOYMENT INSURANCE

Under the 1947 law, unemployment insurance is managed directly by the Ministry of Labour through its network of prefectural and local employment offices, the "Public Employment Security Offices." The provisions of the Unemployment Insurance law are tied to other government manpower services, and include not only cash benefits, but retraining facilities, sickness and injury allowances, and access to a range of welfare facilities.

Coverage

The law includes workers in all firms employing five or more persons, but excludes those engaged in agriculture, forestry, fisheries (except for clerical workers in these industries), seasonal workers, government employees at all three levels. A firm other than these may request voluntary coverage if at least half its workers agree.

About twenty-one and a half million workers were covered in 1972, representing about 42 percent of the labour force, and 64 percent of all employees. Good as this record is, questions must be raised about all those who are not covered, and who must, in time of need, rely on former employers, relatives, or public assistance.

Contributions

Direct contributions to unemployment insurance are equally divided between employers and employees, who pay 1.3 percent of payroll together, or .65 percent each. Day labourers pay a small fixed rate per day. A special extra charge is levied against employers who (for three years running) discharge more than 10 percent of those of their workers who have been employed for at least six to ten months. In addition to employer/employee contributions, the government pays one-fourth of benefit costs (one-third for day labourers) and all administrative costs. In times or areas of extra heavy unemployment, the government's share of the general program also rises to one third.

Benefits

The daily unemployment benefit amounts to up to 60 percent of the worker's daily wage, from a minimum 490 yen a day to a maximum 2,280 yen a day. Given the average wages quoted earlier, this maximum clearly means that the actual benefit for most workers is considerably less than 60 percent of normal pay, and inadequate to maintain an unemployed person's living standard. The duration of benefits varies with length of work and contribution. In general, anyone employed from 6 to 9 months in the preceding 12 is entitled to benefits for 90 days, after a 7-day waiting period. If he has worked at least 10 months in the preceding year, he can get 180 days. Table 8.1 shows other extensions also granted.

If a beneficiary is ill and unable to work for over 14 days, his benefit shifts from unemployment insurance to sickness benefit.

Benefit is extended to cover the entire period up to one year during which the recipient is in a public training program. In addition to unemployment benefit, the person in a training program may receive a

Table 8.1 **Unemployment Benefit Eligibility**

Duration of Work	Duration of Benefit
20 years	300 days
10–19	270
5–9	210
1–4	180

Source: Ministry of Labour, *Labour Administration in Japan*, 1973, p. 31.

"skill acquisition allowance" consisting of an incentive payment for attendance, plus transportation costs. If necessary he may also have a living allowance. All of these taken together may amount to almost 20,000 yen a month: a small amount relative to average wage levels. A small dependent allowance is available, of 2,400 yen a month for a spouse, 900 yen for a first child and 300 yen a month for each subsequent child. Day labourers' benefits are even less adequate. They vary with amount and length of contribution, to a maximum of 17 days at 1,160 yen a day if he has worked 28 days or more in the preceding two months. If he has contributed 11 days a month for a total of 84 days, he may receive up to 60 days' benefit in the next four months.

In 1971 there were 574,000 unemployment insurance beneficiaries with an average total benefit of 28,500 yen (about one month's pay). By 1973 the average benefit had risen to 40,600 yen.[1]

Combined with training and mobility programs, unemployment insurance obviously contains both positive and negative incentives to get work. An unusual positive feature of unemployment insurance is a "start-up" or "outfitting" grant designed to encourage workers to take jobs as soon as possible. If a man finds work while still entitled to at least two-thirds of his benefit period, he is given 50 days' benefit free. If he finds a job with from half to two-thirds benefit remaining, he is granted 30 days' benefit. And if the remaining period exceeds 150 days, he is granted 20 days in addition to either of these two possibilities.

Removal expenses for the family are also paid when a job is found through the Public Employment Security Office.

HEALTH INSURANCE

Organization and Coverage

Health care in Japan is universal; no person is excluded. However, there are differences in benefits and contributions within a rather complex administrative organization. All enterprises employing five or more workers must participate in a compulsory plan, known as "employees' health insurance," with the exception of workers in certain occupations already excluded from unemployment insurance: agriculture, forestry, fishing, catering, and daily or seasonal work where the worker is employed for less than two months. These workers and those in enterprises with fewer than five workers, and the self-employed, may be covered voluntarily in societies or as individuals under a separate national plan. Those who formerly had employees' coverage but are no longer employed may register for "continuing" coverage for a period of one year.

Compulsory coverage of employees is organized within and by a series of employment-based structures. By law, a firm with at least 300 workers may establish a "health insurance society" and those with more than 500 may be required to do so. In practice, the required size of firm is raised to 3,000. Very large companies with different industrial interests or locations may set up more than one society. When a firm is not large enough to set up a society by itself, it may join with others to do so, subject to government approval. In addition to the employer-managed societies, there are special government-operated programs for day labourers and for seamen. Independent "mutual aid associations" are established to cover the national public service, local public service, public enterprises, and private school teachers and employees. Any workers not covered by one or other of these special organizations but who are to be covered compulsorily or voluntarily are included directly within a government-managed insurance program. Finally, the rest of the population (mostly not in the labour force) is covered by a "national" insurance program,

Table 8.2 **Health Insurance Beneficiaries, 1972**

Government-managed	insured	13,095,000
	dependents	12,903,000
Society-managed	insured	10,024,000
	dependents	12,237,000
National health insurance		43,721,000
Day labourers		577,000
Seamen	insured	261,000
	dependents	471,000
National public service	insured	1,155,000
	dependents	1,825,000
Local Public Service	insured	2,622,000
	dependents	3,388,000
Public corporations	insured	785,000
	dependents	1,407,000
Private school employees		204,000

Source: Compiled from Social Insurance Agency, *Outline of Social Insurance in Japan 1973.*

which is, however, managed not as one might expect by the national government, but under government authority by municipalities or by local associations that are not work based. This is for the largest group. Total coverage under all programs in 1972 is shown in table 8.2.

Contributions

Contributions by employers and employees to "employees" health insurance are similar in principle in both the government-managed and society-managed insurance programs. But while the government-managed rate is fixed at 7.2 percent of wages, (shared equally by employer and employee) the societies may vary their assessments up to 9 percent to improve benefits, as long as the employee's contribution does not exceed 4 percent. In 1973, society contributions were on average slightly lower than those in the government-managed program, totalling just under 7 percent, with the employers paying an average of 4 percent and the employees 3 percent. Government gives a small subsidy to societies, and contributes administrative costs plus 10 percent of the cost of benefits in the government-managed program.

"National" health insurance, managed by local authorities, is financed by individual contributions and by heavy government subsidies. Insured persons' contributions are not based on wages, but include a flat rate plus a payment varying with income, family size, and property, to a maximum total contribution of 80,000 yen per year per household. Rates are fixed by local municipalities, and payments are made directly to municipal offices. The charges are very regressive: a family with income under 200,000 yen per annum pays over 6 percent of income, while one with over 5,000,000 yen pays about .6 percent. The general average is about half the maximum. The national government subsidy to this program includes an administrative grant of 606 yen per person (1973), 40 percent of medical care costs, a special grant of 5 percent of medical costs to poor municipalities, and additional direct subsidies to providers of service, both for capital construction and services.

Day Labourers' Insurance was set up in an attempt to compensate for disparities of benefit between casual workers and those regularly employed in companies (especially large firms). Costs are divided three ways. A government subsidy covers 35 percent of the cost of medical care, sickness and injury benefits, and maternity allowances. Employers and employees share equally a daily contribution that varies through four classes of rates of 50, 60, 130 and 200 yen a day respectively. Post office stamps are placed daily on the worker's card to verify eligibility, and the post office then forwards credits to the government social insurance agency.

Seamen's Insurance differs from the other major health insurance plans in that it groups pensions and unemployment benefits with health and sick benefits. The government covers administrative costs, and makes a large flat grant to the insurance fund, as well as contributing one-fourth of the costs of pensions and unemployment. Employers pay an inclusive rate of 15.8 percent and seamen pay 8.2 percent.

A similar blanket coverage characterizes the mutual aid associations of public servants, public corporation employees, and teachers. Since in most cases the government is the employer, there is no separate subsidy. Employer contributions covering medical care, sick pay, invalidity, retirement, and maternity vary among the programs at slightly over 6 percent for long-term employees and 3 percent for short-term. The employee contribution is about 4.4 percent. The exception is the teachers' group, where both employers and employees pay 3.8 percent for both long and short term. In the case of long-term teachers, to make up the shortfall from other societies, the government makes a grant of 16 percent of costs.

Benefits

Medical benefits are similar for all, regardless of the program: treatment, hospital care, drugs, nursing, and transportation costs, for non-occupational illness or injury. Occupational illness or injury is covered by workmen's compensation. For all treatment there is a "partial liability" payment for insured persons of 200 yen for a first consultation, and a token charge of 60 yen a day for hospital care, for the first month. For dependents, the partial liability is 30 percent of the total fee, up to a maximum cost to the patient of 30,000 yen. The cost for dependent care is clearly beyond the means of many workers, underlining the fact that the program is designed only for workers. Dependent costs strike hard at low-wage workers. There is no time limit for treatment or hospitalization. For persons over 70, there is no "partial liability" fee.

A cash sickness benefit is payable to the insured person, to the amount of 60 percent of his "standard remuneration": in effect, his average pay level. There are 35 classes of standard remuneration. Public service employees are treated better than other workers, as they receive 80 percent of wages in sick pay. Single persons in hospital receive only 40 percent of the standard. Sick pay is limited to 6 months' benefit. Dependents may be granted sick pay, depending on circumstances.

Maternity allowance of 60 percent (80 percent for public service employees) is payable to a woman six weeks before and six weeks after confinement. In addition she will receive half a month's salary to cover delivery expenses and a lump sum of 2,000 yen for nursing. Delivery expense for public service employees is a full month's wage. An insured person's wife receives a flat grant of 60,000 yen plus the nursing allowance.

Funeral costs are payable to survivors when an insured person dies, in the amount of one month's wages, with a minimum of 30,000 yen.

All of these benefits are available to all members of the health insurance societies and mutual associations, to seamen, and labourers, and to members of the government programs. Services and benefits in kind are also provided to those covered by national (municipal) health insurance, but the latter does not provide cash sick benefits since persons insured under this program are usually unemployed.

A problem in the sick benefit policy is the limitation to 6 months' benefit. Disability pensions are available only after 3 years, so that there is a considerable lapse of time between eligibility periods in long-term illness. At present this is often made up by employers' policies, which may provide extended sick leave at company expense before the worker takes up his eligibility for sick pay under the insurance program. The three-year waiting period for disability benefits may be reduced on certification by a doctor that the condition is stabilized, or in case of tuberculosis or some other special diseases.

The rates of use, and costs of government-managed and society-managed programs in 1971 are shown in table 8.3.

Society-managed benefits per person were in several areas higher than those received in government-managed programs, but the incidence of cases was lower in all areas, and the major costs of medical care and expenses were lower in societies. Therefore the costs per insured person were lower. This appears to reflect a situation claimed by the societies and acknowledged by government, that facilities and treatment are often of better quality (and more efficient?) in company clinics and hospitals. Further, society members are more affluent, being in larger companies, and presumably do not require as extensive care as those in government programs.

WORKMEN'S ACCIDENT COMPENSATION

Organization and Coverage

Workmen's compensation is operated directly by the national Ministry of Labour through its prefectural offices. Coverage is compulsory

Table 8.3 **Health Insurance, Rates of Use per 1000 Insured, and Costs, 1971**

	Number of cases (per '000' members)		Cost per case (yen)		Cost per insured person	
	Government	Society	Government	Society	Government	Society
Total	6,205	5,242	6,263	5,171	3,886	2,697
Medical treatment	5,813	5,030	5,839	4,775	3,393	2,390
Expense incurred in getting treatment	227	115	4,747	4,560	107	52
Injury benefit	126	71	23,737	25,157	299.2	189.6
Burial	3	1.8	54,281	67,277	15	12
Delivery	13	7.9	17,477	20,544	22	16
Maternity	11	7.2	39,378	49,166	45.7	35.2
Child care	12	7.6	2,000	2,000	2.4	1.5

Source: Ministry of Welfare, Department of Statistics, *Welfare Statistics Handbook 1973*, Tables 218–255, and Kemporen (Federation of Health Insurance Societies) *Annual Report 1971/72*, pp. 96–99.

for all workers in construction, freight-handling, forestry, and fishing (ships from 5 to 30 tons), and for workers in most other industries employing five or more workers. Other firms may be covered voluntarily, except for government services and corporations. In 1972, 27,858,000 workers were covered (slightly over half the labour force) and about 4,700,000 people received benefits.

Contributions vary on the basis of company experience, from .3 per cent to 8.1 percent of payroll. Employers pay the entire cost except for a government subsidy.

Benefits cover work-related injury or illness, including those suffered while travelling to or from work. They include medical care, compensation for temporary disability, invalidity and long-term disability, survivor and funeral benefits, prosthetic appliances, vocational rehabilitation, etc. Compensation for temporary disability lasting over three days, up to three years, is 60 percent of the individual's average wage. Invalidity compensation is for long-term but not disabling consequences of injury or illness. The amount varies with the degree of disability. For some classes the compensation is a pension ranging between 117 and 280 days' wages per year; for others, compensation is paid in a lump sum ranging from 50 to 450 days' wages. Survivor benefits include a pension for dependent members of the immediate family, ranging from 30 percent to 60 percent of the individual's average wage. Long-term disability benefit of 60 percent of wages, plus continuing medical care, is provided if the person is not cured after three years.

PENSIONS

Organization and Coverage

Pensions and retirement allowances are of special interest in Japan because of the important part played by employers. Private retirement plans in the form of annuities are only beginning to become important, but large lump-sum gratuitous allowances have long been an integral aspect of retirement policies. Gratuitous payments have been especially important because the normal "retirement" age from companies is only 55, but public pension systems come into application only at age 65.

There are two major public pension mechanisms. First is an "employees" pension or "welfare annuity" insurance program, covering all employees in "covered working places" employing five or more people. This program is compulsory for these employees and is managed by government, parallel to the government-managed health insurance programs. Others who may be covered voluntarily by employee's insurance are (1) all workers in establishments other than "covered" places (e.g. smaller than 5 persons) as long as more than half agree; (2) individual workers in uncovered places, with the employer's consent; and (3) persons ineligible for any of the above but who, having at least 10 years prior coverage, wish to insure themselves.

The second public pension program is called the "national pension", paralleling the "national" health insurance program. This is divided again, into contributory and noncontributory sections. The contributory scheme is compulsory for all between the ages of 20 and 59 whose income is sufficient to make contributions and who are not otherwise covered, except for spouses of the insured, students, and persons aready pensioned or who were over 50 in 1961. The noncontributory scheme is designed for all those who were unable to contribute to the contributory scheme because of age or low income.

In addition to these major schemes, there is a supplementary Farmer's Pension Fund, again government-administered, designed to give added benefits to all farmers working more than .5 hectares[2] who are already insured under the National Pension. The other publicly approved schemes are those already mentioned under health insurance—for seamen, national and local public service and public corporation employees, and teachers. In all of these, pension and invalidity insurance are part of the plan. Combined coverage of the various plans is very extensive.

Employees' pension funds, like employees' health insurance societies, may be set up as an alternative to government fund by companies employing 1,000 or more persons, or by a group of smaller companies, but only upon consent of at least half the workers and the union. Though growing in popularity, they are not mandatory and have not yet reached the scope of the health societies. In 1973 there were 811 funds with about 4,643,000 members. The main advantage of such funds is that the employers can vary their contributions, to merge with company retirement plans.

Contributions—Employees' Pension Insurance

Contributions vary, with special rates for members of employee pension funds, for women, and for miners. Contributions to both government and company funds combine a flat rate of 5 percent and a

Table 8.4 **Insured Persons, Public Pensions, 1972**

Employees pension insurance	22,514,000
National pension	23,669,000
Seamen	261,000
National public service	1,155,000
Local public service	2,622,000
Public corporations	785,000
Private school teachers, employees	204,000
Farmers' pension	1,016,000

Source: Ministry of Health and Welfare, Social Insurance Agency, *Outline of Social Insurance in Japan 1973*.

wage-related rate. In the government-managed program, the combined rate for men is 7.6 percent of the worker's standard remuneration, shared equally (3.8 percent) by employer and employee. The voluntarily insured person pays the whole amount. The rate for members of employee pension funds is 5 percent, being only the flat rate portion, again shared equally by employers and employees. The usual rates for women are 5.8 percent of standard remuneration in the government funds, and 3.6 percent for employee pension fund members. For miners it is 8.8 percent (5 percent for fund members). The national government also contributes a subsidy of 20 percent of the cost of benefits, 25 percent in the case of miners.

In the employees' pension funds, in addition to the 2.5 percent paid by employees and employers to the government as their shares of the 5 percent flat rate contribution, both contribute an additional 1.3 percent directly to the employees' pension fund (rather than to the government) for a total of 7.6 percent, as in the government-managed programs. But, and this is where advantages come to the large-firm employee, employers may contribute even more, raising the total to as much as 9.6 percent of wages and thereby increasing considerably the pensions of employees of these firms. Employer contributions to employee pension funds may qualify for special tax exemption under what is known as the "tax-qualified pension plan," providing special incentives to employers.

All of these contributions go directly to the government. A reserve fund is accumulated, the interest being available for "social purposes," including 20 percent for local improvements. Of the other social purposes, about 25 percent goes to housing, 13 percent to developing small businesses, and over 11 percent to building homes for the aged. The fund itself amounted to an enormous 434 billion yen in 1973.

Contributions to National Pension

National pensions, being designed for persons ineligible for coverage under one of the employees' pension plans, cannot set a proportion of wages as the contribution base. Instead, a flat contribution is set, of 900 yen per month. Insured farmers too must pay this basic contribution of 900 yen a month, plus an additional 400 yen a month for supplementary benefits. Others may pay 400 yen voluntarily to increase their benefits. The government pays all administrative costs of the contributory plan, plus a subsidy equal to half of the total of all contributions, an additional third of the cost for those whose coverage is by any special provision continued at no charge to them, and 321 yen a month towards farmers insured under Farmers' Pensions. The whole cost of the noncontributory pension plan is carried by the government.

Eligibility and Benefits—Employees' Pension

Old Age Benefits are paid under a series of conditions:

1) To a 60-year-old man (55 years for women and miners) who has 20 years of coverage but is disqualified from further contributions;

2) To a 60-year-old man (55 for women and miners) who has 15 years of coverage since the age of 40 (35 for women and miners) but is now disqualified from further contributions;

3) To a 65-year-old person who has more than the coverage prescribed in (1) and (2) even if he has continued to be insured;

4) To a person age 60–65 who has more than the coverage prescribed in (1) and (2) but whose income is less than 48,000 yen a month;

5) To a person who has more than the prescribed coverage of (1) and (2) but who is disabled by illness after disqualification.

The old age pension benefit consists of a "basic" plus an "additional" amount. The *basic* amount again has two components: (1) 1,000 yen multiplied by the number of months of coverage. In 1973, the minimum was 240,000 yen and the maximum 360,000 yen per year, (running about a third to a quarter of average annual wages). (2) 1 percent of the person's monthly standard remuneration, times the number of months of coverage.

The *"additional"* amount is a supplement for dependents amounting to 28,800 for a spouse, plus 9,600 for each of the first two children, and 3,800 yen for each subsequent child. The combined pension may yield a fairly high percentage of average wages.

Invalidity

Invalidity pensions are payable to those who have at least 6 months' pension coverage but were disabled during the insured period. They are payable upon termination of active treatment for the disability or after three years from the first medical consultation. Benefits are available in three classes depending on the degree of disability, paying, in class I, 125 percent of the basic pension amount plus the supplement, for full disability; in class II, 100 percent of the basic and supplementary amounts, for major disability; and in class III, 75 percent for partial disability, with a minimum of 240,000 yen in all categories. If the insured person recovers within a three-year period, he may receive an allowance instead of a pension. The allowance is a lump sum payment of 150 percent of the "basic" amount.

Survivors

Survivor benefits are payable to dependent members of the immediate family, including parents, spouse, and children, of any person who had been insured at least six months, or was receiving old-age or invalidity pension, or had qualified for it. A husband or parents are eligible only if they are over 60, or disabled, and children only if they are under 18. The benefit for a widow or orphan is half the basic amount plus the additional supplement, and for an adult dependent half the basic amount, with a minimum limit of 240,000 yen plus 9,600 yen for the first dependent child and 4,800 for each thereafter.

All of the benefits as of 1973 are tied to the consumer price index, being adjusted when the index changes by 5 percent or more. Thus the minimum of 240,000 yen was already, by 1974, adjusted upward by 10 percent. Although the minimum was set at 240,000, the national average pension in the employee program was about 600,000 yen per year in 1974.

Withdrawal Grant

Pension equity cannot be withdrawn by a male contributor unless he is over 60 and disqualified to make further contributions. But women may withdraw if insured for at least two years, but disqualified (e.g. through withdrawal from employment). The withdrawal compensation is proportionate to contributions.

National Pension

A full old-age pension is payable at age 65, after at least 25 years' contributions, but the term of contributions is reduced to 10 to 24 years for those who were at least 31 years of age in 1961. Under the reduced requirement, about a million people get 150,000 yen a year. Members of public schemes, spouses, and students may participate voluntarily in the national pension. Survivors' pensions may by this means be increased, if they made contributions during the spouse's lifetime.

The monthly benefit under National Pensions is calculated by multiplying the number of contribution months by 800 yen, and adding one-third of the number of months when the contributor was exempt from contributions, times 800 yen. The formula for the monthly benefit could be expressed as 800 × (no. of months contributed + ⅓ no. of months exempt). There is an annual minimum benefit of 60,000 yen. Considering that the average *monthly* cash income in 1972 was almost 100,000 yen, this annual minimum is obviously little more than token subsistence. Where additional contributions were paid, additional benefits are payable at the rate of 200 yen times months contributed.

Though pensions are normally payable at age 65, benefits may be received any time from age 60 to age 70 with corresponding decreases or increases in the benefit. By the terms of a "coordination" plan of interim adjustment, the above formula applies to persons who by age 65 have contributed at least one year but not enough to purchase a pension.

Invalidity pension under the national pension scheme is calculated in the same way as the old age pension except that total disability provides 125 percent of the pension. Widows with children, or guardians of orphans of insured persons may receive a basic 240,000 yen, plus 9,600 yen for the first child and 4,800 for each subsequent child. A widow without children may receive at age 60 half of her deceased husband's pension.

Noncontributory National Pension is payable at age 70 on a means test to those who are not otherwise covered. However, the means test is generous, allowing an income from other sources of 430,000 yen, plus 90,000 for one dependent or 140,000 for two. The amount of pension is only 60,000 yen a year, evidently in the assumption that some other income is available. A lesser amount may be paid to those under age 70 who are not eligible for any other pension. An invalidity pension of 90,000 yen is payable to a completely disabled person with no insurance coverage, with lesser amounts for reduced disability. Similarly, scaled-down payments are made to widowed mothers (78,000 yen a year plus the supplement for children) and guardians.

Farmers' Pension is designed to facilitate farmers' retirement from active work by benefits predating national pension benefits. A farmer is eligible when he retires from active direction of the farm, after 20 years of contributions. The monthly benefit is 800 yen times the number of contribution months, payable up to age 65, at which time it drops to one-tenth that amount, coordinated with national pension. The period of qualification may be reduced to 5–19 years for anyone over age 36 in 1971.[3] In addition, there is a Farmers' Old Age Pension, which he may receive without retiring, on the same contribution basis as the retirement pension. The benefit is 200 yen times the number of contribution months.

Pension Beneficiaries and Benefits

The figures shown in Table 8.5 do not reflect increases in guaranteed amounts according to policy adopted in 1973. Some are below the prescribed minima now in effect. The real value of contributory pensions as well as coverage, especially of the employee pension program, has risen markedly in recent years. Taking the index at 1970 equal to 100, the consumer price index rose about 23 points between 1968 and 1972. In that time, the number of old-age pensioners in the employee plan rose from 384,000 to 600,000, and the average annual benefit rose from 99,700 yen to 192,800 yen.[4] Even this figure represents only about one sixth of the average full-time wage in 1972. Increases of benefit were not quite so large in invalidity and survivors' pensions, but were of the same order, both in the employees' program and in the other contributory pension plans (public servants, seamen, etc.). Thus recent years have seen real increases in benefits.

Observations may, however, be made in respect to both numbers and benefits. It appears that the employees' pension program still covers only about half the population; this situation may improve in time, but large numbers of people are dependent on very inferior benefits. Six times as many people still rely on noncontributory old-age pension as on employee pension, and more people were added to the noncontributory rolls in the period 1968–72 than to the contributory plans. Beneficiaries in the noncontributory plan rose by 450,000, while the benefit rose only by about 5,300 yen a year (compared with the 93,000 yen increase in the employees' plan), from 18,500 to 23,800.

Though the statutory minima are now the same in employees' pension and contributory national pensions, the disparities in benefits, (especially from the noncontributory benefit), are enormous, greatly in favour of empoyees' pension, especially when it is remembered that

Table 8.5 **Beneficiaries and Average Annual Benefits, Major Pension Programs 1972**

	Employees Pension		National Pension		Noncontributory Pension	
	Number	Average Benefits (Yen)	Number	Average Benefits (Yen)	Number	Average Benefits (Yen)
Old age	600,516	192,800	229,470	52,100	3,670,111	23,800
Coordination old age	139,259	76,800	2,513	20,100		
Invalidity	100,036	148,916	60,116	111,000	395,021	37,900
Survivors	537,547	107,859				
Widowed mothers			126,710	94,600	23,298	31,900
Guardians			92	92,900	122	32,800
Orphans			6,732	65,700		
Widows			4,143	19,200		

Source: Compiled from Social Insurance Agency, *Outline of Social Insurance in Japan 1973*, Tables, pp. 58, 64, 68.

most employees also receive substantial retirement allowances, often equal to three or four years' salary. The same observation is generally true of the invalidity and survivors' programs. In the case of invalidity, far more people must rely on noncontributory pension than those eligible for employees' invalidity pension, yet the benefit is much less.

The discrepancy between employees' pension and contributory national pension is not quite so marked. It is interesting that invalidity benefits in the national pension (both contributory and noncontributory) are higher than old-age benefits, but are lower in the employees' program. In survivor benefits, the great majority are covered by the employee program, and benefits under the national contributory program are not much less than under the employee program. The differences here are between the noncontributory program and the other two.

Another important question is the relation between all of these benefits and average earnings. The general average of monthly wages in 1971 was about 65,000 yen.[5] Even the best pension rate (employees' pension) averages only about 16,000 yen per month, and the lowest (old-age noncontributory) averages less than 2,000 yen a month, which is obviously not enough to sustain the recipient without other public or private aid. Given maturation of the programs, however, it seems that benefits will rise.

An interesting point is that government employees do very much better. The average old-age pension for national government employees in 1971 was 381,000 yen (about 32,000 a month), disability pension was 217,000 yen and survivors' pension 142,000 yen.[6] However, even this is less than half the average wage. Local government employees had even higher benefits, with average old-age pensions of 453,000 yen, disability pensions of 275,000 yen, and survivors' pensions of 169,000 yen. Other mutual association benefits were of the same order as the national government rates.

OTHER BENEFITS

Children's Allowance

Children's allowance is a direct support only to large families, becoming payable only for the third child and subsequent ones. There is a means test, but at such a high level as to exclude only the wealthy, being 3 million yen a year for a family of five. In 1973, 1,947,000 children were recipients. The allowance too is high, relative to such programs as noncontributory pensions, at a rate of 3,000 yen a month per child. Contributions are shared for employed persons by the employer, who pays seven-tenths of the cost, the national government two-tenths while the prefecture and municipality each pay one-twentieth. In the case of unemployed persons, the national government pays four-sixths while the prefecture and municipality each pay one-sixth. The program is unpopular with employers, since in their view wage differentials already take account of family obligations.

Public Assistance

Social assistance policy and rates are set by the national government, but are administered mostly at the local level. Every municipality with 30,000 or more population must have its own public assistance centre. However, 80 percent of the cost of benefits and the cost of administration are borne by the national government. Assistance is strictly a last resort, after all public and family possibilities have been explored, and after wealth and savings have been exhausted. Personal possessions, house, furnishings, are considered wealth. However, the program is open as a supplement to employed persons whose income is below the benefit level. About 80 percent of recipients are aged or handicapped, and public assistance may be used to pay the 30 percent user's liability in the medical care program. It may also supplement old-age or disability pensions, especially in the noncontributory pension program. The assistance rates, in effect, form a kind of national minimum (very minimum) income guarantee. In 1972, there were 1,348,500 beneficiaries. Of these, about 400,000 were under 20 years old, and a similar number were over 60. Benefits in 1974 consisted of a basic rate of 9,450 yen a month. This increased by 1,330 yen a month with each additional family member, plus an age-variable amount for each member. There was also a winter fuel allowance varying by family size and by geographic region. The age-variable allowance ranged from 5,190 yen a month for infants under one, to 14,050 yen for men over 65. The amounts were the same for males and females up to age 14, but thereafter males received about 2,000 yen a month more.[7] Rates are indexed to the cost of living. A typical family of four in mid-1974 might receive 63,700 yen a month in addition to special subsidies for specific purposes such as housing or education costs, as well as full medical care. (This compared badly with average family incomes of over 200,000 yen a month).

A further policy in Japan is that public loan funds are available to low-income people. They may be used for various purposes: to start or support a small business, acquire or renovate a house, for study or school preparation, etc. Altogether almost 9 billion yen were divided among these purposes in 1971, about half of the total being devoted to housing.[8]

WORK-RELATED FRINGE BENEFITS

Striking as are the differences in social security benefits between contributory health and pension programs and the national noncontributory system, they originate in a basic condition of Japanese society: the importance of the job. Salaries determine not only statutory benefits, but also a very important range of nonstatutory or fringe benefits. Although they are nominally voluntary, fringe benefits become the subject of intercompany competition for manpower, of union bargaining, and of national policy. The amount and variety of benefits vary as do wages, with several factors. Foremost is the size of the company (that is, number of employees). Other factors include sex, type of industry, level of education (and level of job), age, duration of service, and family size.

The benefits themselves cover a wide range. Retirement allowances and bonuses are not generally treated as fringe benefits, but as part of what is called "special" wages. Bonuses are much the greater part of this, but together they amount to about a quarter of total cash payments, or almost a third of the amount of "contractual" wages. Other benefits include housing medical care, "livelihood support" (food, clothing, nursery schools, travel costs, bursaries) "mutual aid" (insurance, sympathy gifts) recreation and culture, and various supplements to statutory programs. The voluntary benefits cost the company, on average, 7 percent of all cash payments. Of this, almost half goes to company housing. The statutory programs (pensions, health insurance, unemployment insurance, workmen's compensation, children's allowance) cost 6 percent. The combined bill, then, on average is about 13 percent of all cash costs.

But different industries incurred considerably different welfare costs. In 1973 the heaviest costs were in mining, at 22 percent, and the lowest in publishing, at 9.1 percent. These figures are probably related less to income levels than to work conditions. The mining industry is perhaps necessarily a leader in housing benefits, in sickness and injury compensation, and medical care for its workers, while these needs evidently are not great for a highly urban business like publishing. The percentage allocated to statutory and nonstatutory benefits bears no evident relation to wage levels. The distribution of nonstatutory bene-

Table 8.6 **Average Wages and Benefits, 1973, Selected Industries**

			Percentage of Voluntary Benefits Devoted to:			
Industry	Average of total cash payments	Welfare costs as % of pay	Housing	Medical Care	Livelihood	Other
Communications	200,600	11.2	36.1	8.0	35.1	20.8
Publishing	152,100	9.1	9.0	6.4	56.2	28.4
Precision machinery	130,800	10.5	15.9	8.8	53.1	22.2
Metals	130,800	13.1	48.2	10.6	29.8	11.4
Transport	126,800	10.8	30.7	16.0	30.1	23.2
Mining	117,100	22.0	41.8	28.3	11.6	18.3
Textiles	92,200	14.6	47.0	8.9	23.3	20.1

Source: Nikkeiren (Japan Federation of Employers' Associations), *Report on Fringe Benefit Costs, 1972–73*, pp. 22–24.

fits gives some indication of need peculiar to each industry, as shown in the figures for selected industries.

The Effect of Company Size

Benefits are most likely to vary by company size. Here there is a steady progression upward in totals allocated to housing, in direct relation to company size and therefore also in direct relation to wage levels. There is an inverse relation between company size and the proportion of benefits allocated to "livelihood" benefits. The amounts allocated increase with size even more sharply than the percentage of wage costs, so that workers in large companies get very much better benefits. The effect of company size on major benefits may be examined more closely in respect to specific kinds of benefit.

Housing

Companies have various options: company ownership of housing at low rental to workers, dormitories, and home ownership loans are the main approaches. Of these, by far the largest proportion of cost (between 75 percent and 90 percent) goes on company-owned houses and dormitories, but there is a trend, encouraged by government policy and workers' preferences, towards worker ownership by means of loans. About 78 percent of companies now offer housing loans. The actual amounts spent on housing are, again, directly related to company size. Companies with fewer than 500 employees spent on housing 2,188 yen a month per person in 1973, while those with over 5,000 employees averaged 4,027 yen a month.[9] Most of the large companies offer both company housing for some employees and loans.

Table 8.7 **Effect of Company Size on Nonstatutory Welfare Benefits**

Company Size	Index of Welfare Expenditures
Under 500	100
500–999	115
1000–2999	123
3000–4999	130
Over 5000	140

Source: Nikkeiren (Japan Federation of Employers' Association) *Report on Fringe Benefit Costs, 1972–1973*, p. 16.

Health Care, Food, Recreation

Company health services often work in tandem with the employees' health insurance societies, with which there are contracts for service. But many large companies have their own clinics, and even hospitals, largely limited to use by company workers and their families. In addition, preventive care, recreation centres, rest and vacation resorts, are operated by companies or groups of companies. In some cases such facilities are made available to the community. Most companies of any size also either operate mess halls where noon meals are free or very cheap, or contract to have meals brought in.

Other Financial Benefits

Some other advantages are offered. Many companies offer voluntary benefits for injury or illness not related to work, or sick leave, designed to fill the gap between sick pay and disability benefits. Others give additional survivor benefits or disability supplements. Some offer stock ownership plans, and other loans, for other purposes than housing. Group life insurance is also common. Generally accepted, too, is the practice of paying the daily travel or commuter costs of workers between home and work. Company-issued uniforms are very common.

The influence of company size appears in the statement of the proportions of companies, by size, offering different benefits (table 8.8).

Retirement Allowances

Retirement allowances have traditionally been a very important aspect of company policy, especially since the normal retirement age is 55, while the statutory pensions are not available until age 65. A lump sum payment is usual, though increasingly companies are adopting a pension plan (discussed above) that offers tax exemptions and that is integrated with statutory programs. About half of all companies now give both pension and lump sum. Again, the size of company is critical. Companies with over 1,000 employees make an average contribution to lump sum payments of 4,090 yen a month (1973) while those with less than 100 employees pay only 1,070 yen a month. The annuity pension payment differential is not so large: 770 yen for those over 1,000 and 340 yen for those under 100. Companies will attempt to merge company plans with public plans; thus, one large corporation offers a combined retirement plan as follows: (1) a lump sum of 50 times the monthly salary; (2) a pension plan paying 2.7 months' salary per year; (3) employees' pension (social security) averaging 60,000 yen a month.

Table 8.8 **The Effect of Company Size on Benefits Offered**

Benefits Offered	Percentage of Companies by Company Size				
	Over 5000	1000–4999	300–999	100–299	30–99
Company houses for families	93.9	87.2	64.8	49.5	42.2
Dormitories	89.5	79.6	56.2	39.0	28.8
House loans	93.9	82.2	43.4	25.7	10.8
Company clinics	74.3	43.5	21.2	12.1	3.8
Mess hall	79.2	66.8	53.4	38.6	27.4
Physical training club	95.3	90.5	80.5	70.9	46.5
Health insurance supplement	98.8	80.6	47.7	22.8	14.8
Workmen's compensation supplement	93.6	81.6	59.6	35.2	23.8
Stock ownership	55.3	36.2	13.2	8.5	5.8
Nonhousing loans	84.8	68.8	44.8	30.5	15.6
Home help	28.9	8.9	1.3	.3	.1

Source: Calculated from Ministry of Labour, Statistical Department, *Survey of Welfare Facilities*, 1973.

This total amounts to about 80 percent of the retired person's working salary. If he works he will forfeit all or part of the social security payment, until age 65, at which time he receives it as of right.

The retirement benefit varies with size of company, type of industry, whether the decision was the company's or the worker's, education, service, age, and number of dependents. Taking all industries as a whole, the highest lump sum payment, of nine and a half million yen, would go to a 55-year-old man who took university education before World War II, has served the company for 32 years, has one dependent, and is retiring at company decision. The benefit would be paid on the basis of 40 months' salary. The same man retiring at his own decision would receive only eight and a half million yen. By comparison, a man with high school education but otherwise the same qualifications, would receive 9.1 million if retired by the company, and 8 million at his own decision. At the other end of the scale, a high school graduate aged 21 who has served the company only three years and has no dependents, would receive only 128,000 yen, based on 2.2 months' wages. A man aged 38, with high school graduation, 20 years' service, and three dependents would get 2,788,000 yen, but a woman with the same qualifications, but assuming no dependents, would get only 2,190,000 yen. The relation between company size and benefit is not constant, although generally companies with 1000–3000 employees tend to do better than either larger or smaller ones, especially when the worker decides his own retirement. And companies sized 500–999 often do worse than those under 500. No easy explanation appears.[10]

CONCLUSIONS

It is clear that wages, social security, and other benefits all show the effects of Japan's adherence to a capitalistic economic structure. Wages, social security, and fringe benefits are all directly related to the sex of the worker, the size of company, and type of industry. Furthermore, nonworkers' benefits are very much less than those of workers. Government manpower policy relies on a high employment rate, and efficient placement and training services, along with limited unemployment benefits that must, on the whole, act as strong incentives to work.

Health services as such are a major exception to differentials of treatment, but even here large firms tend to offer better health care to their workers than is available to the general public. Sick pay, accident compensation, invalidity, survivors' and old-age pensions are all calculated on the basis of work history and wages, resulting in important continuing differentials among industries even for fully employed men. The differences among fully employed men, women, casual workers, and unemployed persons are even more marked. National contributory and particularly noncontributory pensions are below minimum maintenance levels. Even though new programs are introduced or old ones are improved, these industry-based differences continue.

Politically, there is no visible force that will change the existing patterns, since trade unions are enterprise-based and do not take action to extend benefits to nonworkers (even though this goal is given recognition by the largest labour federation, Sōhyō). The allocation of resources is, apparently, determined by the very large and affluent corporations, whose lead is necessarily followed by smaller ones. Their choices are given preference by the government, which acts as a residual agent to provide benefits for the less fortunate. Individual roles are primarily economic, man as producer and consumer, and not political. Mechanisms at prefectural and municipal levels for the administration of manpower services, or social benefits, are government-directed even where there is token representation by consumers and workers. The result appears to be an efficient production machine, leaving little option for alternative roles for "the little man."

Part 5

Conclusion

CHAPTER NINE

Powers and Benefits: A Comparison

COMPARING GOALS

Three countries have been described with respect to their social benefit programs, in the expectation that these programs would express the perspectives accepted in those countries about the proper distribution of goods and social roles. Two main positions were theoretically anticipated: contractual and individualistic, or systemic and collective. We have noted that all three countries tend to look for collective solutions, even though there are wide differences in the structures expressing their collective goals, and corresponding variations in the public acceptance of differences in levels of income or social class. These general orientations were examined in respect to two focal areas: first, attitudes about work, and the organization of work and incomes; secondly, the administrative processes of benefit programs relative to political attitudes and processes.

The three countries have been described in particular through examination of four main aspects of social programs: coverage, eligibility, contributions, and benefits, because each says something about individual or collective responsibility. They also give an indication of attitudes about the principle of equality in the distribution of benefits and costs.

David Gil suggests that "the processes of resource development, status allocation, and right distribution are the key variables or key mechanisms of all social policies." He goes on to point out that these sets of variables thus become the major points of attack not only for policy analysis, but also for improvements in policy.[1] Gil further divides "rights" into rewards and general entitlements. Rewards (and punishment) represent contractual perspectives, while entitlements represent rather systemic acceptance of need as sufficient ground for collective action. Both of these principles may be found in policies affecting salaries, social security benefits, taxes, and social assistance, and conditions on their use, such as coverage and the terms of eligibility.

In all three countries work is accepted as the basic condition of eligibility for full participation in the rewards of social security. The rewards, or benefits, generally vary both with the duration of work (and number of contributions) and with the amount of contribution, based on salaries earned at work. When work is not the criterion, and the basis of allocation shifts from rewards for work to entitlement as a member of society, the benefits reduce markedly. This seems to be a world-wide situation with noncontributory pensions or with social assistance, or (as in the case of sick benefits for Yugoslav farmers or Japanese nonworkers) benefits are simply unavailable. It is only as a nation increases its resources, and if national goals include reduction of disparities in distribution—and as the nation learns how to effect that distribution—that it can diversify and extend programs to non-workers beyond the level of basic subsistence. The provision of universal health care is a major step in all three countries towards a shift from rewards to entitlements and towards equalization of benefits, but this does not yet extend to cash sick benefits. Undoubtedly, the absolute level of benefits is directly related to the level of resources in the nation. But a better indicator of adequacy is the relative level of benefits to wages, and in this regard both Yugoslavia and Sweden make a better showing than Japan.

The consensus of democratic thinking is to assign higher value to systems that have wide coverage, that reduce the range of disparity of benefits, and that distribute statuses and roles among many people, rather than the converse of these trends. Yet it is acknowledged that this value system may not, at least in the short run, necessarily result in better distribution of goods, security or sense of self-fulfillment, than programs that allow wide disparities or are centrally managed. The Japanese seem to experience a sense of gratification in national achievement, and to be prepared for personal sacrifice for the sake of collective goals. It is hard to say that gratification of individual needs, or equalization of benefits, have greater ultimate value to them than has collective achievement. Their collective goals accept hierarchical distributions, while those of Sweden and Yugoslavia aim for equalization.

It is rather hard to make exact comparisons among countries on measures of reward; that is, of coverage and adequacy of benefits. Even the easily quantified components of goods-distribution are not quite comparable because statistics are prepared by each country for its own purposes and in recognition of specific issues that concern that country. For example, Japanese statistics on rates of use and levels of benefit are commonly organized according to size of firm (number of employees), while that element gets little attention in Sweden and Yugoslavia. In Yugoslavia, the differences among republics are of prime interest for policy development, but obviously have no parallel in Japan, while Sweden's counties are not of major significance to policy-making. In Sweden, differentials of age, sex, and marital status are of more concern than they are in Yugoslavia.

It is even harder to make comparisons about user participation, or the issue of role allocations, because little attention has been paid in social security literature to this aspect of administrative policy, while other literature on social policy or administration has largely ignored role-assignment processes in social security, though there is a great deal concerning politicians, managers, and bureaucrats.

However, it is evident that Yugoslavia's central preoccupation for thirty years has been with the problem of allocation of power and responsibility, not only in industry but also in social management. This concern has reached its fullest expression in the 1974 Constitution, that more clearly than ever before sets out the framework for self-management in all aspects of Yugoslav life. Sweden's attention to the same issue has been of much longer duration, and is by now firmly institutionalized in programs that seek to maximize the benefits for society as a whole and minimize the differences of benefit and opportunity among citizens. Expectations of egalitarian attitudes and behaviours are well defined, and promote the central objectives of equalization. At the same time, there are indications that the processes that have assured equalization of benefits in Sweden have not satisfied aspirations for distribution of roles. Indeed the essential central bargaining relationships among owners, workers, and government may not permit wide distribution of roles, but this very issue is now being raised by radical worker representatives.

Japan presents what might be described as a double picture. The democratic ideals of equalization and self-determination are often expressed, but the supporting institutions of elected governments, non-government societies and active trade unions are overlays on a tradition of the alliance of central bureaucracy and paternalistic relations in privately owned industry. Rewards are increasingly gained and distributed, but even more evidently than in Sweden, this process proscribes equalization of roles. The three countries form a continuum of the democratic concept, in a very general way, ranging from Japan where democracy is a formalistic addendum to historically vertical social, political, and economic structures, through Sweden where democracy is already firmly defined and fiercely defended in these three types of structure, to Yugoslavia, where the limits of democracy in political, economic, and social affairs are not yet fully conceived, as its variations may reach into the lives of all citizens.

COMPARING BENEFITS

Despite these differences of political perception and expression, it is not possible to say that one country is "better" or even "better off" than another, except by the measure of one's own values, or by reports of satisfaction of the people concerned. Even when social indicators are developed that can accurately measure total life experience, the questions of preference remain.

In regard to the material aspects of social benefits, it has appeared that there are more similarities than differences among the three countries. In the area of *health*, all have assurances of universal health care, dental care, and hospitalization, with special provision for work-related injuries or illness. All apply small user charges for health care. All also have cash sickness benefits for insured workers including support for women during pregnancy and postnatal care. The rates of cash benefit vary. In Sweden, full compensation may be up to 90 percent of the worker's average wage, while in Japan and Yugoslavia the amount is about two-thirds. But all are designed to maintain the approximate standard of living of the worker, to protect him or her from major indebtedness, and to protect his or her rights to other future social benefits (such as pensions). Whether the purpose of these programs is to protect the individual's right to health care or to assure the return of a healthy work force is in itself not the issue. In all cases, income support is directed primarily to the worker. The nonworker is in general not covered. This issue is of major importance in Yugoslavia since the uninsured peasants form an important segment of the population.

Sweden has gone farthest in trying to extend cash sick benefit coverage to nonworkers, (or to extend the concept of work), in such programs as unemployment benefit for uninsured workers, sick benefits for the "spouse-at-home" or pay to parents of sick children, and in national and municipal housing allowances. On the other hand, Yugoslavia uses the "solidarity fund" to equalize resources among workers, to reduce disparities in benefits resulting from regional differences in productivity. Both Sweden and Japan use government grants for this purpose.

In the area of *pensions*, again, all countries make basic provision for retirement, for disablement, and for surviving families. Here the distinctions between the benefits available under contributory and noncontributory "national" pensions show up in Japan and Sweden, highlighting a major policy issue that equalization policies and contribution-based insurance "equities" are incompatible. Up to what point is it "fair" to allow contributors to assure their personal retirement incomes (and so to perpetuate the disparities already created during their working lives)? The same problem exists for all these countries, as in sickness benefits, in the calculation of benefits as a percentage of income, since the same percentage necessarily creates disparate results. Sweden now handles the problem by making all benefits taxable (at a stiff rate) and arbitrarily setting a maximum pensionable income of seven-and-a-half times a basic minimum. In Yugoslavia, for better or worse, the problem of contributory or noncontributory pensions does not arise, because all pensions are paid for from work organizations.

Because of the complexity of formulae in each country, it is hard to compare actual benefits; all are trying to raise rates, and Yugoslavia seems to set a high goal of about 70 to 85 percent of the individual's rate of pay.

A different problem in Japan has been the ten-year gap between retirement age and pension age. The Japanese government has tried to reduce the effects of that uncovered period by encouraging companies to raise the age of retirement, and to participate in the shift from lump-sum to annuity retirement payments.

The principles in manpower policy and unemployment insurance are the same for all countries, though Yugoslavia's decentralization seems greatly to reduce the effectiveness of its manpower programs. Unemployment compensation is not widely used in Yugoslavia, partly perhaps because full use of the program would expose the exclusion of many workers from full social participation that is hard to reconcile with the principle of community, partly because of traditional reliance on the extended family as a source of support, but also because of sheer lack of funds and lack of jobs. One of the difficulties in a decentralized society is the absence of a coordinated labour market, or machinery for its development. In Sweden and Japan, on the other hand, it appears that job placement is paramount, in the interests of the worker as of the nation, and centrally controlled manpower programs are highly efficient and contain a wide range of incentives to work.

About 80 percent of Swedish workers are covered for unemployment insurance, and benefit rates go as high as 90 percent of the individual's wage. In Japan, only 42 percent of the labour force is covered and benefits range only up to about 60 percent of wages. Unemployment compensation thus reflects real differences among the three countries in their ways of dealing with nonworkers.

Housing is also very indicative of the nation's philosophy about the place of the worker in society, for in Japan financing and planning are primarily the business of the firm, in Sweden of the state, and in Yugoslavia of the commune or local community. Sweden goes farthest in extending this important resource to nonworkers, using housing grants of many kinds to reduce disparities in people's living conditions.

PARTICIPATION AND POWER

In these and other programs discussed in more detail above, the financial arrangements for benefit programs are indicative of assumptions about the responsibility of actors in society. In Yugoslavia, contributions for both rewards and entitlements are largely assessed entirely against the enterprise, as the collective economic base of the community. Decisions about investment in production, as against wages or against social benefits must be made by workers collectively, in a variety of roles as producers, as union members, as local residents, as consumers of social or health services. Social benefits are embedded in society as a whole, and economic decisions are at the same time political decisions. For better or for worse, the individual is one of the community.

In Sweden, economic power has been recognized as the domain of employers, while the social interests of the workers and increasingly of nonworkers, or citizens at large, are represented by unions and achieved politically. There is a structured conflict between employers and unions, moderated by the state (when it wishes, with a bias towards the workers). Contributions made by individuals are, in a sense, the price of assuring their right to a share in decision-making in social policy. In fact, unions are now pursuing even harder the extension of political participatory democracy into economic democracy, or shared decision-making in the firm. But ownership is still private, not collective, and the community to which the citizen must look is not the local but the national community, with the state acting as the conscience and agent of the people. Many Swedes have long since adopted the goal of unifying economic and social policy though the structures of unification are not worked out as they are in Yugoslavia. It occurs now at the national, rather than the community level.

Characteristically, in Japan, large firms are encouraged (even compelled) to manage health insurance and pensions for their workers, within guidelines established by governments that are ever mindful of the necessities of economic growth. Government programs are residual, becoming less generous as the beneficiary is distant from employment in a large firm. Except for those most remote from that happy status, the unemployed and destitute, contributions for most programs are shared by workers, employers, and the state. While minimal security is thus assured by the state, contentment is not; the individual is in danger if he is not within the shelter of the firm which is the "community". There is, in short, unity of political, economic, and social policy resting on the dominance and success of big business.

This situation has not raised serious difficulties, because of Japan's rapid increase in production, in real wages, and in standards of living. Perhaps if there had been less loyalty to the firm there would have been less success. One can only guess at the responses of the state if the situation should arise that the firm cannot fulfil its social duties to its workers. Meanwhile, the behaviour of both employers and workers suggests that the assignment of responsibilities and rights is satisfactory to both, that the state has made the appropriate decisions regarding those assignments and its own role of efficient supervision, that despite a rather wide range of inequities in benefits and a concentration of power at the top, these conditions are acceptable since roles are at least clearly defined and assured.

MODELS FOR CANADA?

Reference was made earlier to Heclo's conclusion that the bureaucracies are probably the agents in each country most responsible for the direction taken by social policies, and for borrowing between countries. In Canada, the influence in the policy process of deputy ministers and senior civil servants has steadily increased over recent decades.[2] It is also clear that the need for governmental control over social policy becomes inescapable as society becomes more complex: that, as P. E. Trudeau said, "The future of Canadian federalism lies clearly in the direction of cooperation"[3] among levels of government. What is the cooperative future of Canada? Is it possible to envisage collectivist principles similar to those of any of the three countries discussed here? The place of the bureaucracy is important as we move towards collective forms. It seems important to consider not only what kinds of goals we wish to achieve and how those goals are established, but also the mechanisms of administration, that is, the place of the bureaucracy relative to the political structures, and the place of consumer citizens in relation to both. If borrowing among nations is, as suggested above, the way countries develop their social benefit programs, and yet having regard to the ways special characteristics of each country are exemplified in their programs, is it possible to identify aspects of the programs of these three that might be borrowed by a country like Canada? First, what about the distribution of political and administrative power?

Sweden established its reputation long since as a kind of exemplary welfare state that has, however, retained its capitalist base and its parliamentary government. Heclo could find no special political reason why any particular reform took place when it did or under the political leadership of the time rather than under other circumstances; but, as he observed, Sweden's programs often predated and outran those of other countries.[4] Before the major reforms undertaken by the Social Democratic Party over the past forty years, Sweden had had widespread unemployment and was much behind the industrial leaders in economic development and standard of living. There is no doubt that there was an effort to pull themselves up by their own bootstraps. They used their own traditional institutions as instruments for the control of policy and of the bureaucracy towards the achievement of collective goals. Sweden, in effect, set itself to a heroic effort to bring a better life to its people, and has followed that determination since.

The same can be said of both Japan and Yugoslavia. In this regard, Japan has been one of the economic wonders of modern times, bringing itself in thirty years from destruction and disorganization close to the economic leaders among modern states. Its social benefits seem to follow as an incidental reward for effort rather than as a reason for economic success. They have been ahieved by tight discipline in business as in public administration, and by coordination of the two. Yugoslavia, by comparison, has made social benefits an integral part of its political and economic development, dictated by the necessities of federal cooperation.

All of these changes involved or were facilitated by a degree of political change following crisis. The Yugoslav change was, of course, the most radical, and has resulted in the most radical re-thinking of the relationship of the individual to the state. The emphasis on local autonomy and self-management has no parallel in the modern world,

among western capitalist nations, among the Soviet bloc, or among
the developing nations. Yugoslavia is a federal nation, for the very
good reason that its member republics need each other if they are
to maintain their independence from external powers, but none wishes
to be dominated by the others. Its local autonomy springs from the
same motives. So strong is this principle that the entire Constitution
was written to express the primacy of the locality over the centre.
Instruments then had to be found to bind the parts together. Such
an arrangement becomes thinkable for Canada, given the unquestioned
"fact" of Quebec, and the constant struggle for power between the
federal government and the provinces.

Constitutionally, both Japan and Sweden are unitary parliamentary
states and seem to have little novel to offer as models for a federal
Canada. Yet Sweden's political and administrative structures are both
of interest. The assignment of administration to boards in Sweden
creates a separation of political and executive responsibility, yet re-
tains accountability of the administration both directly to the Riksdag,
and even more immediately to the people at large through the representative composition of the boards. By this process and other machinery for public accountability such as the use of consultative "remiss"
procedures, the public access to state documents and the ombudsman
position, Sweden involves her people in political issues more widely
than is possible in Canada. Such institutions as *remiss* and the ombudsman role have been strongly urged in Canada by Donald Rowat.[5]

The Canadian system concentrates political and administrative
power in the cabinet, and it appears that politicians like to believe
that (to quote Lyndon Johnson) "having the power, they have the
duty."[6] But the responsibility too is awesome. It would not be impossible to borrow some of the Swedish procedures, in particular to
create public service boards, by development and modification of
crown corporations, that already resemble Sweden's administrative
boards. Indeed the suggestion has already been made in Canada
that the Post Office, for one, be incorporated, and it is not difficult
to contemplate assignment of provincial health care programs and
federal/provincial pensions and family allowances, to boards. Such
boards at the provincial, or even municipal levels, would then no
doubt negotiate (as they do in Yugoslavia) for transferability of benefits between jurisdictions.

Such boards could certainly relate to governments at the local and
provincial levels, as well. In Canada, local school boards have been
a possible example. Unfortunately their powers have been progressively reduced by provincial ministries of education. But many provincial governments have, in recent years, carried out special studies

of ways to create regional governments, strengthen municipal government, or set up metropolitan areas. It seems not at all unreasonable to give them real work to do, as is done in Sweden, for example, by assignment of health services to county governments.

Another area that merits exploration is the central emphasis given in Yugoslavia, and increasingly in Sweden, to the true nature of "contributions" to social insurance programs, as taxes. As taxes, and as collective rather than individual responsibilities, they are levied in Yugoslavia against the enterprises rather than the individual worker. This does not lead to wide abuse of benefits. To the contrary, as we have seen, coverage and eligibility are often more limited than is the case in other countries. Similarly, benefits are closely controlled; health care calls for user charges. Social "insurance" is more symbolic than real in Canada, since government must underwrite the funds in any case. Apart from the use of individual contributions as taxes, individual records are kept as instruments of control of eligibility. In Yugoslavia, as in Canada, a personal work record is kept as a basis for estimating benefits, but the tax is quite appropriately recognized as such, and not designated misleadingly an "insurance premium."

In Yugoslavia, workers participate in decisions about the amounts of contributions (and benefits) they wish to pay or be paid. The same occurs in Sweden through national agreement between the L.O. and the Swedish Employers' Federation, as far as the supplementary programs like superannuation benefits are concerned. These agreements are also heavily influential in the framing of laws and public regulations through the participation of these bodies in policy-making. In Canada the same process occurs around fringe benefits, but only through the tough process of collective bargaining that sometimes leads to disastrous consequences for the general public. No doubt, it will be argued that in Canada governments and bureaucracies can give better assurance of consistent service than woud be the case if such matters were left either to local governments or to union negotiations. And no doubt that is indeed the case at present, given the traditions of union-management self-interest and the fact that local governments, employers, and unions have not been given opportunities to manage such affairs under modern conditions. But the examples of Sweden and Yugoslavia suggest that the financing of social programs is a form of taxation, and that those who pay (employers and workers) should not be excluded from the decisions.

In Canada, it has been assumed that such questions are best left to politicians. Politicians are thus burdened with a great many issues on which they have no expertise. For this they depend on their bureaucrats, and both are inclined to centralize and maintain their powers. There is every reason to diversify and distribute the political functions by creating new political roles in human services equivalent to those public corporations already proliferating in the administration of industry or communications. These would include not just those general-purpose politicians elected to legislatures or municipal councils, but also persons who would represent the (political) interest of contributors and users on boards with specific policy-making and administrative powers far beyond those now given to advisory boards in Canada. This objective was at the heart of structures set up by Quebec following the (Castonguay) Commission on Heath and Social Welfare. Unfortunately Quebec was not able to take serious action to implement the true spirit of the proposals, since it was at the same time engaged in the effort to establish its provincial identity. The decentralist spirit was in conflict with the attractions of centralist efficiency, and the regional health and welfare councils were not given the means to be effective.

Yugoslavia has not yet satisfied itself on the problem of coordination of effort and resources that is necessary to weld together the many fragments of autonomous bodies, but the system of delegation upwards, uniting political, social, and economic policy looks promising. Sweden, in contrast, has found ways to moderate highly centralized power by delegation both sideways and downwards to boards, employers, unions, and county governments. Canada is more united than Yugoslavia, yet cannot be unitary like Sweden. Some of the political forms of both countries may well be examined and borrowed by Canada.

The Japanese situation is peculiar to that country, politically, racially, and culturally homogeneous and unitary as it is. The regional and ethnic competition found in Canada does not exist. Though people often seem driven to desperation by the narrowness and indeed the tragedy of the roles they play in society, they somehow are sustained by the very limitation of alternatives. In such a situation, it is possible for a devoted and relatively uncorrupted public service corps to pursue collective solutions. The solutions are found through the domination of private corporations; so powerful and pervasive are the corporations that they become in fact instruments of national policy. This pattern is not open to imitation by Canada, but does constitute an alternative, especially for homogenous nations of the Third World.

What about the distribution of benefits? What lessons are there for Canada? As observed above, programs may be designed to provide a bare subsistence, on the ground that recipients are an unfortunate burden on a productive society; or they may be designed to maintain recipients at their customary level, or even at the level of the average for the whole society, on the ground that they have been or will again be productive, and that in any case indignity and suffering demean the whole society; or they may, for a small number, be designed to raise the recipients far beyond the normal level, in the expectation of great things, or in reward of the past (as for example retirement allowances for members of parliament).

Like all of the countries under study, Canada offers all three kinds of program, but the main social benefit programs do not attempt to maintain normal living standards, nor to equalize incomes. The failure of Canadian income support programs to effect transfers from one income class to another has often been noted.[7] Sweden approaches equalization by several routes: one is a very steep progressive income tax; another is the setting of an arbitrary base income, and a maximum of seven-and-a-half times that base for contributions and benefits in several programs; a third is the provision of a variety of almost universal benefits for housing and other services that are standard for people of all incomes; another is a high rate of cash benefit during sickness, extending some benefits to the "spouse at home", parents' pay for care of sick children, and unemployment pay for uninsured workers. All of these programs, while they do not necessarily redistribute incomes, do help to equalize the standard of living, and prevent very low-income people from undue discrimination.

Yugoslavia also offers sick pay, but otherwise the programs are not unlike Canada's. There is a conscious effort to equalize incomes and benefits, and despite some regional disparities in both, these are not so great as to require income redistribution programs, beyond the very interesting use of "solidarity funds" at all levels. The two main areas of interest in Yugoslavia's programs are the system of enterprise-based financing of all social programs, including education and housing, and second, the multiple political procedures that link the world of work to the rest of society.

Japan is of interest to Canada not because of differences in government programs, but because of the very prominent part taken by industry in providing and operating a great range of benefits and services, from pensions and health insurance through to such important details as housing, work clothing, and commuting tickets. As in Yugoslavia, the economic unit similarly assumes responsibility for many aspects of workers' lives, so that the work milieu is also a community. Large Japanese firms provide medical facilities, housing, recreation, and many other benefits that make workers anxious to "belong" to that company. Membership is not decided, as in Yugoslavia, by co-workers, but by owner or managers; but the outcome of a many-faceted attachment is similar. Both countries contrast sharply with the sense of alienation experienced by many Canadians, whose work is so widely separated from other aspects of their lives.

The major question of social policy, then, seems to be not whether work now conditions the forms and amounts of social benefits, for it does; but how political and economic power relate to each other, and how the worker relates to both, as contributor and as policy-maker. The form of relationships of structures carrying these powers and their legitimacy in the historical understanding of the people, determine the form of social services and will determine whether and how services are extended beyond workers to nonworkers, how wide will be the range of benefits within categories of workers and nonworkers, and whether and how workers and nonworkers will be involved in decisions about these basic social questions.

NOTES

CHAPTER 1

1. Leonard Marsh, *Report on Social Security for Canada* (Ottawa: Advisory Committee on Reconstruction, 1943).
2. *The Commission of Enquiry on Health and Social Welfare.* Vol. V, Tome II, Quebec Official Printer, 1971.
3. Hugh Heclo, *Modern Social Politics in Britain and Sweden* (New Haven: Yale University Press, 1974).
4. An excellent recent example is Peter Kaim-Caudle, *Comparative Social Policy and Social Security* (London: Martin Robertson, 1973).
5. Harold Wilensky, *The Welfare State and Equality: Structural and Ideological Roots of Public Expenditure* (Berkeley: University of California Press, 1971).
6. These are the major items examined in reports of the International Social Security Association.
7. This observation is clearly confirmed by Harold L. Wilensky, *The Welfare State and Equality: Structural and Ideological Roots of Public Expenditure* (Berkeley: University of California Press, 1975). But as he recognizes, social security spending levels are affected by other factors than affluence; notably, by the age of the program and the size of the pension population.
8. Daniel Bell, *The Coming of Post-Industrial Society: A Venture in Social Forecasting* (New York: Basic Books, 1973), p. 115.
9. See for example: Leonard Marsh, *Report on Social Security for Canada, Income Security for Canadians* (Ottawa: National Health and Welfare, 1970); Peter Kaim-Caudle, *Comparative Social Policy and Social Security* (London: Martin Robertson, 1973).

CHAPTER 2

1. Brian Chapman, *The Profession of Government* (London: Allen and Unwin, 1959), p. 18.
2. International Labour Organization, *Income Security in Europe in the Light*

of Structural Changes (Geneva: *Second European Regional Conference*, 1974).
3. Taken from Erik Karlsson, *Democratization and Reorganization* (Stockholm: Swedish Confederation of Trade Unions, 1974), Mimeo.
4. The National Insurance Act, revised translation (Stockholm: July 1972).

CHAPTER 3

1. Official Statistics of Sweden, *Income and Wealth Statistics* (1971), Table 1, p. 11.
2. Source: Ministry of Labour and Housing, *The Structure of Incomes in Sweden* (Stockholm: 1970), Mimeo.
3. Jan Nasenius et al, *Social Assistance in Sweden* (Stockholm: Ministry of Welfare, 1972), Table 39, p. 74.
4. Alva Myrdal, *Towards Equality* (Stockholm: Prisma, 1971).

CHAPTER 4

1. Ministry of Labour and Housing, *Swedish Labour Market Policy* (1973), Mimeo.
2. The best summary of social insurance, from which much of this material is taken, is published by Trygg Hansa, *Social Benefits in Sweden* (Stockholm: 1973–74).
3. The exchange rate is roughly 5 kr. to $1. (U.S.).
4. Source: Official Statistics of Sweden, *National Insurance* (1971), Table 2.15c.
5. Ibid., Table 3G.
6. Ibid, Table 4C.
7. See report that the LKAB strike "was aimed less against the employers than against the trade unions" in M. Donald Hancock, *Sweden, The Politics of Postindustrial Change* (Hinsdale: Dryden Press, 1972), pp. 164 ff.
8. Swedish Institute, *Current Sweden* (December 1974) No. 54.

CHAPTER 5

1. Source: *Yugoslav Statistical Yearbook* (Belgrade: 1973), Table 104–1.
2. About 15 dinars per $1. (U.S.) in 1974.
3. Taken from *Yugoslav Statistical Yearbook* (1973), Tables 220–2, 220–3.
4. Taken from Federal Institute for Statistics, Statistical Bulletin, 799, *Survey on Family Budgets of Workers' Households* (Belgrade: 1973).
5. Ibid., Table 2–1.
6. Ibid, Table 2–2.
7. Ibid, Table 2–1.

CHAPTER 6

1. *Yugoslav Statistical Yearbook* (1973), Tables 104–12, 13.
2. Personal Communication, Community for Employment, Ljubljana.
3. Personal Communication, Community for Health Insurance, Ljubljana.

4. Source: Federation of Communities for Pension and Health Insurance, "Review of Basic Social Insurance for 1972" (Belgrade: 1973), Tables A25, 28, Mimeo.
5. Calculated from Federation of Pensions and Health Insurance, "Review of Basic Social Insurance for 1972", Tables A5, 9, 14, 31, 31, B9, 10, 32, 39, 42.
6. *Yugoslav Statistical Yearbook* (1973), Tables 123–4.
7. Personal Communication, Lek Pharmaceutical Co., Ljubljana.
8. *Yugoslav Survey* XIV, No. 2 (May 1973) p. 89 et seq.
9. Taken from Federal Institute for Statistics, Statistical Bulletin, 799, *Survey on Family Budgets of Workers' Households*, Table 2–1.
10. Howard M. Wachtel, "Workers' Management Interindustry Wage Differentials in Yugoslavia," *Journal of Political Economy* 80, No. 3, Part 1 (May/ June 1972).
11. See for example Ana Barbic, "The Differences in Participation of Men and Women According to Republic," in *Socio-Political Participation in Local Communities* (Ljubljana: University of Ljubljana, 1973).
12. Stane Saksida et al, "Social Stratification and Mobility in Yugoslav Society," in *Some Yugoslav Papers Presented to the 8th Congress*, International Sociology Association (Ljubljana: University of Ljubljana, 1974).

CHAPTER 7

1. Bank of Japan *Economic Statistics Yearbook* (1973 $1.00 (U.S.) = about 300 yen), Table 145.
2. *Yearbook of Labour Statistics* (1972), Table 120.
3. Ibid.

CHAPTER 8

1. Source: Ministry of Labour, personal information.
2. 1 Hectare = 2.47 acres.
3. Social Insurance Agency, *Outline of Social Insurance in Japan* (1973).
4. Source: *Japan Statistical Yearbook* (1972), Table 334.
5. Source: Ministry of Welfare, *Statistical Handbook* (1973), Table 251.
6. Source: Ministry of Welfare, *Statistical Handbook* (1973), Table 259; *Japan Statistical Yearbook* (1972), Table 334.
7. Source: Ministry of Welfare, *Assistance Rates* (1974), Mimeo.
8. *Japan Statistical Yearbook* (1972), Table 329G.
9. Source: Nikkeiren (Japan Federation of Employers' Associations), *Report on Fringe Benefit Costs* (1972–73), p. 25.
10. Source: Kanto Management Association, *Report of a Computer Model of Retirement Allowances* (1974).

CHAPTER 9

1. David Gil, *Unravelling Social Policy* (Cambridge, Massachusetts: Schenkman, 1973), p. 17.
2. See J. E. Hodgetts, *The Canadian Public Service, A Physiology of Government* (Toronto: University of Toronto Press, 1973).

3. P. E. Trudeau, "The Theory and Practice of Federation", in Frederick Vaughan et al, (eds.), *Contemporary Issues in Canadian Politics* (Scarborough: Prentice-Hall, 1970).

4. Hugh Heclo, *Modern Social Politics in Britain and Sweden* (New Haven: Yale University Press, 1974).

5. See Donald C. Rowat (ed.), *The Ombudsman* (Toronto: University of Toronto Press, 1965); and "The Problem of Administrative Secrecy", *International Review of Administrative Sciences*, 32, No. 2, 1966.

6. For a careful discussion of the growth of executive power in the cabinet, and the functions of the civil service, see J. E. Hodgetts, *The Canadian Public Service*.

7. Most often quoted is Canada, Senate, Special Committee on Poverty, *Poverty in Canada* (Ottawa: Information Canada, 1971).

BIBLIOGRAPHY

Sweden

Allardt, Erik, and Hannu Uusitalo, "Dimensions of Welfare in a Comparative Study of the Scandinavian Societies," *Scandinavian Political Studies* 7 (1972).

Bostadsstyrelsen (Housing Board), *Facts About Housing* (Stockholm, 1973).

Carlson, Bo, *Trade Unions in Sweden* (Stockholm Tidens forlag, 1969).

Elder, Neil C. M., *Government in Sweden* (Oxford: Pergamon, 1970).

Engström, Martin, *Employment Injury Insurance in Sweden* (Stockholm: National Social Insurance Board, 1969).

Erici, Bernt, *Unemployment Insurance in Sweden*, series *To Our Foreign Readers* (Stockholm: National Labour Market Board, 1970) (mimeo).

Hancock, M. Donald, Sweden: *The Politics of Post Industrial Change* (Hinsdale: Dryden Press, 1972).

Johansson, Sten, *Conceptualizing and Measuring Welfare* (Stockholm: University of Stockholm, 1972) (mimeo).

Korpi, Walter, *The Welfare Poor in the Welfare State* (Stockholm: University of Stockholm, 1972) (mimeo).

Lagerström, Lennart, *Social Insurance and Private Occupational Pensions in Sweden* (Stockholm: Swedish Staff Pension Society, 1971).

Lagerström, Lennart, AGS (Sick Pay Insurance for Workers) and STP (Complementary Pension Insurance for Workers) (Stockholm: Swedish Staff Pension Society, 1972).

Lindblom, Rolf, *The New Style Factories* (Stockholm: Swedish Employers' Confederation) (mimeo).

Meidner, Rudolph, and Öhman, Berndt, *Fifteen Years of Wage-Policy* (Stockholm: Swedish Trade Union Confederation, 1972).

Ministry of Finance, *The Swedish Economy 1971–75. The 1970 Long-Term Economic Survey* (Stockholm, 1971).

———, *The Swedish Budget 1973–4* (Stockholm, 1973).

————, *Outcome of the Standard Medical Fee Reform in Sweden* (Stockholm, 1972) (mimeo).

Ministry for Foreign Affairs, *National Dental Insurance Plan Proposed* (Stockholm. 1972) (mimeo).

Ministry of Health and Social Affairs, *National Insurance Act* (Rev. 1972).

Myrdal, Alva, *Toward Equality* (Stockholm: Prisma, 1971).

Ministry of Labour and Housing, *The Structure of Income in Sweden* (Stockholm, 1970) (mimeo).

Ministry of Labour and Housing, *Swedish Labour Market Policy* (Stockholm, 1973) (mimeo).

Nasenius, Jan. *Socio-Political Reform Policy During 1970–73—An Account of the Facts* (Stockholm: Ministry of Health and Social Affairs, 1974) (mimeo).

Nasenius, Jan, Erikson, Ingerman and Ritter, Kristina, *Social Assistance in Sweden* (Stockholm: Social Welfare Department, 1972) (mimeo).

National Board of Health and Welfare, *Nature and Objective for the Care of the Aged* (Stockholm, 1971) (mimeo).

National Labour Market Board, *Swedish Employment Policy* (Stockholm, 1973).

National Labour Market Board, *Labour Market Training in Sweden* (Stockholm, 1972) (mimeo).

National Labour Market Board, *Labour Market Policy 1974–75* (Stockholm, 1973).

National Social Insurance Board, *Swedish National Pensions* (Stockholm, 1973) (mimeo).

National Social Insurance Board, *Social Security in Sweden* (Stockholm, 1974) (mimeo).

National Swedish Board of Education, *Labour Market Training* (Stockholm. 1970) (mimeo).

Navarro, Vicente, "Methodology on Regional Planning of Personal Health Services: A Case Study: Sweden," *Medical Care* 8, No. 5 (September–October, 1970).

Nordic Council, *Yearbook of Nordic Statistics* (Stockholm, 1971).

Norr, Martin et al, *The Tax System in Sweden* (Stockholm: Skandinavska Enskilda Banken, 1972).

Official Statistics of Sweden, *National Insurance 1971.* (Allman Försäkring 1971) (Stockholm: National Social Insurance Board, 1973).

Official Statistics of Sweden, *Income and Wealth Statistics, 1971* (Inkomsoch förmögenhet, 1971).

Official Statistics of Sweden, *The Cost and Financing of the Social Services in Sweden in 1971* (Stockholm: National Central Bureau of Statistics, 1972).

Official Statistics of Sweden, *Statistical Abstract of Sweden.*
The Swedish Association of Local Authorities (Stockholm: Association of Local Authorities, 1973).

SAF, Swedish Employers' Confederation (Stockholm: Swedish Employers' Confederation, 1972).

Swedish Employers' Confederation, *Non-Wage Labour Costs in Sweden 1974* (Stockholm: SAF, 1975) (mimeo).

The Swedish Institute, *Active Manpower Policy in Sweden, 1972.*
Current Sweden 54 (December, 1974).

General Facts on Sweden, 1973.
Local Government in Sweden, 1972.
Maternity Benefits to Become Parenthood Benefits, 1973.
The Organization of Medical Care in Sweden, 1971.
Social Insurance in Sweden, 1973.
Swedish Industry, 1973.
The Swedish Job Security Act, 1973.
Taxes in Sweden, 1973.
Swedish Trade Union Confederation (LO), *The Trade Unions and the Family* (Stockholm: Prisma, 1973).
Trygg Hansa, *Social Benefits in Sweden, 1973* (Stockholm: Trygg Hansa, 1974).
Wengström, Sten, *National Sickness Insurance in Sweden* (Stockholm: Försäkringskasse forbundet, 1971).

Yugoslavia

Association of Health Institutions of the Socialist Republic of Croatia, *Health Act, and Act on Health Insurance and Obligatory Forms of Health Care for the Population* (Zagreb, 1972).
Blagojević, Borislav T. ed., *Collection of Yugoslav Laws* (Belgrade: Institute of Comparative Law).
———, VIII, Constitution of the Socialist Republic of Serbia, 1964.
———, XII, Statute of the Commune of Pozarevac, 1965.
———, XIII, Laws of Enterprises and Institutions, 1966.
———, XVI, Laws on Employment Relationships, 1967.
———, XX, Law on General Administrative Procedure, 1969.
Dragić, Nada, ed., *Drugi Kongres Samoupravljača Jugoslavije* (Le Deuxième Congrès des Autogestionnaires de Yougoslavie) (Belgrade: Medzunarodna Politika, 1972).
Fisher, Jack C., *Yugoslavia, A Multinational State—Regional Differences and Administrative Response* (San Francisco: Chandler, 1966).
Himes, Richard S. et al, *Organization and Description of Health Services in a Commune* (Washington, D.C.: Association of American Medical Colleges, Student Projects/DIME, 1972).
Kosir, Martin, *The Kranj Commune* (Belgrade: Medzunarodna Politika, 1966).
Institute of Sociology and Philosophy, University of Ljubljana, *Some Yugoslav Papers Presented to the 8th World Congress of International Sociology Association* (Ljubljana, 1974).
University of Ljubljana, *Drujbenopolitična Aktivnost Občanov u Krajevni*

Skupnosti (Socio-Political Participation in Social Communities (Ljubljana, 1973).

International Labour Office, *Workers' Management in Yugoslavia* (Geneva, ILO, 1962).

Meister, Albert, *Ou Va l'Autogestion Yougoslave?* (Paris: Edition Anthropos, 1970).

Pusić, Eugen, ed., *Participation and Self-Management*, First International Sociological Conference on Participation and Self-Management (Zagreb: Institute for Social Research, University of Zagreb, 1972).

Questions Actuelles du Socialisme, "Accord d'Autogestion du Combinat 'Acieries de Sisak'," No. 114 (août, 1973).

Savez Zajednica Penzijskog i Invalidskog Osiguranja Jugoslavije i Savez Zajednica Zdravstvenog Osiguranja Jugoslavije, (Federation of Communities for Pension and Disability Insurance and Federation of Communities for Health Insurance of Yugoslavia), *Pregled Osnovnik Podataka Socijalnog Osiguranja za 1972 Godinu* (Review of Basic Social Insurance for 1972), (Belgrade, 1973).

Socijalistička Federativna Republika Jugoslavija, Savezni Zavod za Statistiku (Socialist Federal Republic of Yugoslavia, Federal Institute for Statistica), *Anketa o Porodičnim Budžetima Radničkih Domačinstava U1972 Statistički Bilten 799* (Survey on Family Budgets of Workers' Households in 1972, Statistical Bulletin #799), (Belgrade: Federal Institute for Statistics, 1973).

Socialist Federal Republic of Yugoslavia Sluzbeni List 8 Maja 1969, #20, 291 (General Act Respecting Health Insurance and Compulsory Forms of Health Protection for the Population, dated 26 April 1969). Translation Geneva, International Labour Office, Legislative Series 1969 – Yug 2.

Statisticki Godišnjak Jugoslavije 1973 (Yugoslav Statistical Yearbook, 1973).

Socijalistička Federativna Republika Jugoslavija (Socialist Federal Republic of Yugoslavia), *Sluzbeni List, 6 July 1972, #35* (Law on Basic Rights in Pension and Invalid Insurance).

Socijalistička Federativna Republika Jugoslavija (Socialist Federal Republic of Yugoslavia), *USTAV* (The Constitution of the Socialist Federal Republic of Yugoslavia), (Ljubljana: Dopisna Delavska Univerza, 1974).

Wachtel, Howard, "Workers' Management and Interindustry Wage Differentials in Yugoslavia," *Journal of Political Economy* 80, No. 3 (May-June 1972).

Yugoslav Survey, "Adjustment of Pensions to Economic Trends," 13 (May, 1972).

————, "Local Communities," 13 (August, 1972).

————, "Housing and Housing Construction," 13 (November, 1972).

————, "Housing," 14 (May, 1973).

Japan

Titles marked * are translations of texts only in Japanese.

Dōmei (Japanese Confederation of Labour), *Welfare Indicators of Workers* (Tokyo, 1972).

Dore, Ronald, *British Factory-Japanese Factory* (London: Allen and Unwin, 1973).

Economic Planning Agency, *White Paper on National Life 1973* (Tokyo: Economic Planning Agency, Japanese Government, 1973).

Economic Planning Agency, *Basic Economic and Social Plan* (Tokyo: Economic Planning Agency, Japanese Government, 1973).

Economic Statistics Annual 1973 (Tokyo: Statistics Department, Bank of Japan, 1974).

Japan Statistical Yearbook 1972 (Tokyo: Japanese Government, Office of the Prime Minister, 1973).

Japanese National Committee, International Council on Social Welfare, *Social Welfare Services in Japan* (Tokyo: Japanese Committee, ICSW, 1973).

Kantō Keieisha Kyōkai (Kanto Management Association)*, *Report of a Computer Model of Retirement Allowances* (Tokyo: Kantō Keieisha Kyōkai, 1973).

Kempōren (National Federation of Health Insurance Societies)*, *Annual Report 1972* (Tokyo: Kempōren, 1973).

Kempōren (National Federation of Health Insurance Societies)*, *Health Insurance and Health Insurance Societies in Japan* (Tokyo: Kempōren, 1973).

Ministry of Finance, *An Outline of Japanese Taxes* (Tokyo: Tax Bureau, Ministry of Finance, 1973).

Ministry of Health and Welfare, *A Brief Report on Public Health Administration in Japan* (Tokyo: Ministry of Health and Welfare, 1972).

Ministry of Health and Welfare, *Children's Allowance Law of Japan* (Tokyo: Children and Families Bureau, Ministry of Health and Welfare, 1972).

Ministry of Health and Welfare, *White Paper on Health and Welfare* (Tokyo: Japan Institute of International Affairs, 1972).

Ministry of Health and Welfare, *The Significance and Background of Problems of the Aged* (Tokyo: Japan Institute of International Affairs, 1973).

Ministry of Health and Welfare, *Welfare Statistics Handbook 1973*,* (Tokyo: Department of Statistics, Ministry of Health and Welfare, 1974).

Ministry of Labour, *Summary of Report on Employer Welfare Facilities** (Tokyo: Statistical Department, Ministry of Labour, 1973).

Ministry of Labour, *Japan Labour Laws* (Tokyo: Ministry of Labour, 1968).

Ministry of Labour, *Yearbook of Labour Statistics* (Tokyo: Statistics and Information Department, Ministry of Labour).

Ministry of Labour, *Labour Administration in Japan* (Tokyo, 1973).

Ministry of Labour, *Basic Employment Measures Plan* (Tokyo, 1973).

Ministry of Labour, *Annual Report of Unemployment Insurance 1972** (Tokyo: Employment Security Department, Ministry of Labour, 1973).

Mitsubishi Trust and Banking Corporation, *The Tax Qualified Pension Plan* (Tokyo: Mitsubishi Trust and Banking Corporation).

Nihon Rōdō Bunka Kyōkai (Japan Labour and Culture Association), *Health and Security Times Monthly**, No. 819 (25 March 1974).

Nikkeiren (Japan Federation of Employers' Associations), *Nikkeiren News*, No. 52 (February 1974).

Nikkeiren (Japan Federation of Employers' Associations), *Report on Fringe Benefit Costs 1972/73** (Tokyo: Nikkeiren, 1974).

Organization for Economic Cooperation and Development, *Manpower Policy in Japan* (Paris: OECD, 1973).

Social Insurance Agency, *Outline of Social Insurance in Japan 1973* (Tokyo: Social Insurance Agency, Japanese Government, 1974).

Sōhyō (General Council of Trade Unions of Japan), *White Paper on Wages for 1974* (Tokyo: Sōhyō, 1974).

Sōhyō (General Council of Trade Unions of Japan), *This is Sōhyō* (Tokyo: Sōhyō, 1972).

Yakabe, Katsumi, *Labour Relations in Japan* (Tokyo: International Society for Educational Information, 1974).